WILLIAM SHAKESPEARE PUNCHES A FRIGGIN' SHARK AND/OR OTHER STORIES

Here's something that all the chumps who skipped over the small print missed: some amazing shark facts! Did you know that gestation period among sharks ranges from five months to two years? Two years spent being pregnant! That's bonkers. Some other species of shark, like the sand tiger shark, practice intrauterine cannibalism, in which the first embryo to reach about 10cm in length then eats all their smaller and less-developed siblings, while still inside the uterus. Then when the siblings are all gobbled, the embryo goes on to eat the mother's unfertilized eggs, all before birth. That is, I believe, objectively even more bonkers!

ISBN-13: 978-1-936561-49-0

Printed in Canada
10 9 8 7 6 5 4 3 2 1

Cover Art by Chip Zdarsky

Interior designed by Emily Horne

This is a work of fiction. Actually, it's a book containing a work of fiction, but you get the idea. Incidentally, did someone file this book in the "Choose One's Own Nonfiction Adventure" section? Bad news on that front, friend: names, characters, places, and incidents in this work either are the product of the author's imagination or are used fictitiously, and any resemblance to actual persons, living or dead, businesses, companies, events, or locales is entirely coincidental! Except for Shakespeare. He's real. He probably definitely did all the stuff in this book, too.

To sharks...
...or not to sharks.

WELCOME

discerning and attractive reader of interactive fiction, and congratulations! You hold in your hand the most advanced Shakespeare simulator on the market today. In it you will find the fruits of untold millions of hours of research performed by the world's greatest Shakespeare scholars, all aimed towards a single goal: finally, at long last, understanding the mind of the greatest writer the English language ever produced.

But even with all those generations of painstaking and often tedious work, there are still huge blanks left in Shakespeare's history. We don't know what all those Shakespeare scholars have been doing, but it sure hasn't been filling in when Shakespeare was born, where he went to school, what he studied, where he worked before writing plays, or what he was doing from 1564 to 1582 and 1585 to 1592 inclusive. They've also managed to lose track of precisely what he looked like, what he wrote, what he didn't, when most of his plays were actually performed, and even, in a few cases, THE ACTUAL PLAYS THEMSELVES.

Great work, Shakespeare scholars.

As such, I have been forced to fill in those blanks with what our I assure you are my last, best, and most informed guesses. This story is presented in a branching, "choose your own path" format, for a very good reason: where there were disagreements over what happened in the historical record between myself and the researcher's historical consensus, both options are presented, with the wording carefully weighed so that the option chosen by most people when reading corresponds to the likelihood of that option being the historical truth. It's all very scientific, and extremely complicated.

I am very proud to present the fruits of this labour here, and I invite you to sit back, relax, and enjoy the most accurate and educational trip back in Shakespearean England (then called "England") available today.

Please enjoy *William Shakespeare Punches A Friggin' Shark And/Or Other Stories*.

RYAN NORTH
TORONTO, 2017

1 You are William Shakespeare! You have been born, done a bunch of things which you definitely remember clearly but which you certainly don't want to get into here, and are now an adult trying to get work as a playwright here in England. History will record that you have but two goals in your life:

> 1) become the greatest author of all time, and
> 2) punch a friggin' shark.

The catch is, punching a shark seems fraught with danger and death, while becoming the greatest author of all time just means sitting alone in a room and writing until your stories don't suck anymore. Which will you focus on first? What will your destiny be, William Shakespeare?

• Write *Hamlet*: Turn to 2
• Go punch a shark: Turn to 13

2 You write *Hamlet.* It's a bit long, but it's pretty good. You were, uh, "inspired" by an existing work, but you're in an era before intellectual property is a thing, so who cares? Nobody! In fact, you're so stoked about *Hamlet* that you just might write another play.

• Write *Romeo and Juliet*: Turn to 3

3 Done! This play is also excellent, and yeah, you did kinda crib from an existing work, but all's well that ends well.

Hey, that gives you an idea!

• Write *All's Well That Ends Well:* Turn to 4
• Go punch a shark: Turn to 14

4 Done! ANOTHER excellent play, Shakespeare. This may not come across as eloquent as you'd put it, but the sentiment is sincere: you are the #1 best guy at writing plays good.

In fact, you're so inspired by your most recent work that you decide to write a bunch more new plays, including *The Tempest, Two Gentlemen of Verona, The Merry Wives of Windsor, Measure for Measure, The Comedy of Errors, Much Ado About Nothing, Love's Labour's Lost, A Midsummer Night's Dream, The Merchant of Venice, As You Like It, The Taming of the Shrew, Twelfth Night, The Winter's Tale, Pericles: Prince of Tyre, The Two Noble Kinsmen, King John, Richard II, Henry IV: Part 1, Henry IV: Part 2, Henry V, Henry VI: Part 1, Henry VI: Part 2, Henry V:, Part 3, Richard III, Henry VIII, Troilus and Cressida, Coriolanus, Titus Andronicus, Timon of Athens, Julius Caesar, Macbeth, King Lear, Othello, Antony and Cleopatra*, and *Cymbeline*.

Whew!

That took you your entire professional life!

But you're not done yet! You write even more! You blast out 154 sonnets (126 to a young man, 28 to a woman) and there's some real winners here, actually. "Shall I compare thee to a summer's day?" NOT BAD, SHAKESPEARE. Whoever the guy is that you wrote that about is, he must have been really something!

Anyway, after that you write a few long-form erotic poems and are about to call it a day when suddenly you think: hey, I'm William Gosh Darned Shakespeare. I've written a bunch of plays that everyone at least pretends to enjoy, I've made up words like nobody's business, and people quote me like whoah. I've written tons of gay poetry, a few hetero poems for the straights, and even done punch-up on other writers' scripts. I'm established, I'm professional, and I'm at the peak of my game.

"I'm finally ready," you think. "At long last, I have the skills required to graduate to that most difficult form of literature, wieldable only by a civilization's most advanced wordsmiths." You stare at the quill on your desk, your fingers trembling as you reach to pick it up, certain that the next few moments are about to begin the most challenging task of your entire career.

This time you speak out loud.

"I'm finally ready . . . "

• " . . . to write one of those choosable-path adventures, where the reader gets to decide what happens next." Turn to 5
• " . . . to punch a friggin' shark!" Turn to 15

5 Yes. YES. Stories where only one thing happens and it's the same thing every time are entry-level baby stuff. You're going to write a story where THOUSANDS if not MILLIONS of things can happen, and it can be different every time you read. But what will it be about?

You go for a walk to get inspiration. You're rambling along a beautiful country road in autumn, deep in a yellow wood, when the road diverges into two, going off into the distance in opposite directions. You stand there for a long time, suddenly keenly aware of how much you wish you could take them both. You look down one as far as you can, but there's a bend in the road, and you can't see where it goes. You look down the other one and it's just as pretty, but there's also no clues as to where it leads either. You agonize over your decision, somehow certain that if you could only take the road less travelled by, it would make all the difference.

"Wow, someone should totally write a poem about these roads," you think.

Eventually, after agonizing indecision, you decide:

• Go left: Turn to 6
• Go right: Turn to 17

6 You walk down the leftmost road, and it's pretty good! The other road was probably way worse. You definitely made the right choice and don't regret this road at all.

A little ways down you come across a man dressed as a court jester. From that, you deduce that he probably IS a court jester. In fact, as you consider the man, you realize you can deduce a lot by just carefully observing what you see in front of you. The fact he's wearing his jester clothes outside the court suggests something's gone wrong with his job.

Has it switched to seasonal hours? No – the clothes are dirty, stained, worn out. He's been wearing them constantly: they're his only clothes. He was fired, an ex-jester down on his luck. You're marvelling at how much you can learn from tiny, apparently insignificant details.

"Someone," you think, "should write a story about an eccentric man whose greatest talent is his deductive reasoning. He could live here in London as some sort of consulting detective, accompanied always by his sidekick, while his opposite, a consulting criminal, would use his equally-great mind to pull off heists." You're beginning to get excited. "This consulting detective could help out the police on their most difficult cases. He could wear a signature hat when he's solving crimes. He could also," you reason, "do drugs."

Your train of thought is interrupted as the man speaks, and unfortunately you forget the idea forever. Oh well!

"I'm a court jester who has been fired from his job a while back," the man says, confirming your suspicions.

"Hello", you say.

"Are you William Shakespeare?" he says.

"I am," you say.

"Hey, here's a story for you," the man says. "How about a story where a court jester gets fired from his job, so he goes to live in the woods, and then he holds up famous playwrights at swordpoint and takes all their money."

You think it's a bad idea for a play, but as he pulls out his sword and holds it to your neck, your mind is already racing. Court jesters! Of course! In your play *Hamlet*, you had a character, "Hamlet", dig up the skull of one of the jesters from when he was a kid, and then think out loud about how gross dead bodies are. People went crazy for that. What if you wrote a PREQUEL story, all about that jester, but with the twist that unlike most choosable-path adventures, in this one you HAD to die?

"Oh, wow," you think, as you give the jester all the money you have. "This is definitely the book I want to write!"

"This isn't much money," the jester says.

• Tell him writing doesn't pay that well: Turn to 7
• Tell him all that glistens is not gold, thereby quoting your own work to him: that always wins over strangers: Turn to 18

7 "Writing doesn't pay that well," you reply. "Even for me, William Chucklesworth Shakespeare."

"I didn't know that was your middle name," the jester says.

"It definitely is, even if future scholars suppress all evidence of that name because they without exception all believe it's the worst middle name they've ever heard of across all space and time," you reply. And then you run home to write your new story.

"Wait, come back!" shouts the jester. "I wasn't done robbing you!!"

• Go home and write your new book about your Yorick the Court Jester character: Turn to 8
• Go back and be robbed: Turn to 19

8 A few weeks later, you're done, and your first choosable-path adventure is finished. You're really happy with it! It's got intrigue, it's got mystery, and it's definitely got the reader dying on every second page. In fact, you're so happy with it that you go over to your artist friend's house and show him your new story, and on the spot he sketches out illustrations to go with each ending and passes them to you.

They're great! You're holding them in one hand in admiration. Your other hand is behind your back, surreptitiously crumpling up the stick figure sketches you'd already made in your own time. You can now see that they're completely horrible. Every single one had Yorick labelled with an arrow that said "YORICK (that's YOU!!)".

You've now learned that real artists don't do that.

"Your style is so futuristic," you say, continuing to admire your friend's artwork.

"Thank you," he says. "It's my idea of what art will look like in the far off year of 21,550,294."

"That's probably too far," you say. "People will probably draw like this sooner than that."

"Nah," he says.

A few months later, the printer returns with the first copies of your new book. "As you know," he says, "each copy of this book was coloured by hand, as we don't yet have the technology to print books in full colour affordably here in Shakespearean England."

"That's fine," you say, "because I wasn't worried about that. It's probably functionally the same anyway."

• Examine your book: Turn to 9

9 It's terrific. The printing came out great, the illustrations "kick butt" (that's a phrase you just invented), and it definitely features a court jester who is destined to die so that your play, *Hamlet*, can take place. You're extremely satisfied with the work.

Unbeknownst to you (Shakespeare), but beknownst to you (the player) because I'm telling you now, all copies of your new book carry a terrible curse. On the way here the delivery person cheesed off a witch, accidentally relieved themselves in a cursèd graveyard, unknowingly awoke some ancient evils and equally-unknowingly trapped them in this text (it was a very eventful trip over from the print shop) and long story short: if you die in the book, Shakespeare, YOU DIE IN REAL LIFE. I thought it only fair to warn you. Now I know it, and you (the reader) know it, but Shakespeare, the character who you're currently controlling, does not. But don't worry: this is a form of dramatic irony – which all research indicates Shakespeare himself was a big fan of! – so he wouldn't be upset. The dude loves irony!

Okay! Do you, William Shakespeare, want to read this copy of your new book?

• Well I don't see why not: Turn to 34
• Hmm for no particular reason, maybe let's not read books right now: Turn to 10

10   "I, William Shakespeare, do not want to read this book I just wrote," you say. "In fact, I am going to destroy all extant copies of it, which is why any future generations won't know I wrote a story in which you can play as Yorick and make fart noises to entertain a small child."

"In retrospect," you continue, "that's probably for the best, actually."

You rush to the printer, buy all his copies off of him, and burn them. There: curse avoided, if there even was a curse, which, of course, you as William Shakespeare can't say!

As you stare at the flames devouring your latest book, the strangest mood comes over you. You wanted to write a non-linear second-person adventure, and you did. You feel like there's nothing you can't do now. In fact, things that previously seemed impossible now seem entirely within reach. You've become the world's greatest author: so great, in fact, that you're now burning your own books JUST BECAUSE YOU CAN. There's only one thing left for you to do to secure your legacy.

"Think I'll go punch a shark," you mutter.

• Go punch a shark: Turn to 11

11   You travel to Buckingham palace for an audience with the King. "I would like to punch a shark," you say to King James, the second regent to ascend to the throne in your lifetime. "It is important to me that I do this. I have but two goals in my life, and the first one has already been achieved. This, my liege, is my final challenge."

"You are one of our greatest playwrights," the King says, "and I will help you. Go forth, and punch a shark."

"Oh," you say. "I . . . I was hoping you'd help me find one."

"I actually have way more important things to do," says the King. "I run a whole country. But you may now punch a shark with my blessing."

You bow. "Your majesty," you say, and you leave, a little disappointed but also very excited. Your lifelong dream of punching a shark can finally be realized, and with the King's blessing!!

You rush home, and . . .

• Go study sharks: know thy enemy: Turn to 28
• Go out to sea to see if you can meet some: go meet thy enemy: Turn to 58
• Decide to stay on land for the rest of your life: I'm gonna hang out here in case my enemy shows up: Turn to 12

12

"Yes," you think. "I will remain here in England, lest any shark ever p ull itself onto land, it shall find me there standing sentry against the beast, punching any such 'land sharks' back into the cursed sea from whence they came."

Your duty is an endless one, but you welcome it. Every day you go for a walk. Every day you look to see if any sharks have tried to colonize the last great undiscovered country (for humans it's death, but for sharks it's clearly land). And every day no sharks attack. Eventually, your body begins to fail you. You have no regrets: you've written some amazing stuff, had some cool kids with an amazing woman (oh, P.S. you had some cool kids with an amazing woman during this adventure, it was happening in the background of the other scenes and I just didn't mention it), and lived the best life you can. You did just fine, William Shakespeare.

You go to your grave having never punched a shark, but also having never allowed any sharks to walk around on land like they're people, probably using their tail fins as feet. And for untold generations after you die, people continue to quote your beautiful words, including "All the world's a stage, and all the men and women merely players" (*As You Like It*, Act 2, Scene 6), "Men at some time are masters of their fates: the fault, dear Brutus, is not in our stars, but in ourselves, that we are underlings" (*Julius Caesar*, Act 1, Scene 2), and "Here is my butt" (*Othello*, Act 5, Scene 2).

THE END

13 You travel to Buckingham palace for an audience with the Queen. "I would like to punch a shark," you say to Queen Elizabeth. "It is important to me that I do this."

"You are but one of our many playwrights," the Queen says, "and still at the start of your career. I will not help you. Go forth, and write some better plays, perhaps some that flatter us, and we may consider your petition in the future."

You leave disappointed and angry. On the way out you try punching a wall to relieve your anger, but it's a stone wall, and now your hand is broken. That's the hand you write with, Shakespeare! You totally weren't ready to punch a shark, and now you can't write plays either!

You try writing plays in your non-dominant hand, but nobody can read them. Finally you hire your pal, Christopher Marlowe, to transcribe your plays for you as you dictate them. But then instead of giving you the credit, he takes all the credit himself. That's right: all of Marlowe's plays were secretly written by you!

"If only," you think, "if only I had not tried to punch a shark so early in my life, perhaps I could've lived longer while still punching a shark later, and also become famous for writing cool plays."

But alas, it's too late for that. You morosely attend a dinner party a few nights later and are stabbed to death in a dispute over the bill.

P.S. This is the worst ending in the book and you got it right away! Maybe just flip back to the start when nobody's looking, and then the fact that you lost at reading a book on your first turn will forever be OUR SECRET.

14 You decide to take a break from writing for a bit, and instead find work on an oceanic sailing ship. It's hard work, but it makes your muscles look awesome, and one day, out at sea, you spot a school of sharks.

"I have already clearly indicated my odd yet lifelong obsession with shark-punching," you mutter, stripping down to your underwear so you can dive into the ocean and fight a shark for no reason. "So what I, William Shakespeare, am doing here makes sense both dramatically and character-wise."

Unfortunately for you, when you dive into the water and punch a shark, it bites you in half, which attracts other sharks, and soon you are torn to shreds. A few of your bones escape the feeding frenzy and sink to the bottom of the ocean, where they feed the blind animals that dwell in that eternal, highly-pressurized darkness.

And that's the end of you, Shakespeare! Your name, however, is taken by a consortium of other playwrights, who use it to produce some of the most famous writing in the English language. They credit all the plays to you, because you had conveniently done the legwork of establishing yourself as a writer, and then, equally conveniently, disappeared under mysterious, shark-based circumstances. And the worst part is that nobody will ever know the truth!

Sucks to (briefly) be you!

THE END

15 You decide to take a break from writing for a bit, and instead find work on an oceanic sailing ship. It's hard work, but it makes your muscles look awesome, and you are excited to return to England because when you do you'll be both the greatest AND most ripped author of all time!

One day, out at sea, you spot a school of sharks.

• Finally! My well-established shark-punching obsession can reach its climax! EXAMINE SHARKS: Turn to 31
• Naw. Return to England, super ripped, and write more plays! Turn to 16

16 You ignore the sharks, and the next time your ship returns to England, you and your muscley body hop off and get back to writing.

Sadly, writing is not hard physical labour, and your muscles fade back to normal almost instantly. Seriously, it's like it happens overnight. Turns out you only get to keep your muscles for as long as you use them!

"Working out is a total scam," you whisper, your eyes finally open to the truth, "and nobody should ever do it."

You mourn your muscles, and then get back to your writing. It was a choosable-path thing you wanted to write, yeah?

• Write a choosable-path adventure: Turn to 5

17 You walk down the leftmost road, and it's pretty good! The other road was probably way worse. You definitely made the right choice and don't regret this road at all.

A little ways down the road you come across a woman selling pies. You feel like you could go for a pie, so you buy one from her. They cost more than you expect.

"Highway robbery," you say.

"Naw, that's the other path," says the pie seller. You chat with her for a bit longer, and she seems really familiar.

"You know what," you say, "you remind me of my character "Sam Ampson", from my famous play *Romeo and Juliet*!

"I'm sorry?" she says.

"*Romeo and Juliet*! It's a play that I, William Shakespeare, wrote," you say. "Two surprisingly young teens fall in love, get into trouble, commit suicide, and the whole thing is over from start to finish in about 4 days of in-story time?"

"I'm not sure I know it," says the woman.

"Come on!" you say. "Remember? Everyone acts like it's this great romance, but the older you get the more you realize that Romeo and Juliet's parents were absolutely correct, and they shouldn't have been allowed to see each other, because the second they got together all they did was RUIN EVERYTHING and then DIE?"

"I don't really get out much to the theatre," she says.

"Well," you say, "you gotta check out the Globe. It's great! Only the most expensive tickets get chairs, so if you've ever wanted to stand on your feet for an entire play, you can't miss it!" You press a two-for-one coupon for the Globe into her hands.

"Thanks," she says.

You walk away, happily munching your pie, when suddenly inspiration strikes. That's it! Of course! You've written SEQUELS to your books before, but never PREQUELS! And certainly never both at the same time! What if – WHAT IF – you could somehow write a choosable-path story that was both a SEQUEL to *Hamlet* and a PREQUEL to *Romeo and Juliet*? And it could star famous tertiary character Sam Ampson!

You rush home and begin to write.

• Write book: Turn to 88

18 "All that glistens is not gold," you say, quoting your own play *The Merchant of Venice* to the jester/robber. He knows you're quoting your own work, and you do too. It's not cool. It's really awkward and embarrassing.

• Look to the jester for his reaction: Turn to 33

19 You stop your escape, and instead, return to the jester who was robbing you.

"I'm sorry," you say, "for trying to escape. But now, AGAINST ALL LOGIC, I have returned for you to continue your robbery of me."

The jester puts his blade to your neck.

"Wait!" you say. "Doesn't my return make you feel good? Doesn't that make you want to not rob me after all? That's kinda how I saw this going!"

• Look to the jester for his reaction: **Turn to 33**

20 You try, through sheer force of will, to die. And it turns out you actually have an innate skill at this! I'm serious, you're like the world's #1 prodigy at willing yourself to die, but you'd just never tried to do it before. Anyway, it goes great, and you die real fast. Bam! Just like that. Kapow!

Your body is buried in a shallow grave, and 25 years later it's dug up by this guy, Hamlet! In this version of reality he's digging for gold and all he's found is skeletons.

"Alack me," he says, "another dang ol' skeleton. Nasty."

He throws your skull back and long story short it turns out there's not a lot of gold in this graveyard! This sucks for Hamlet but doesn't really affect you as a dead dude too much, the end!

THE END

Well there's not really a line so much as there is "a bunch of people all milling about in a cold room" but you push your way in to the front of it. There are people in your way, but you literally push them out of the way.

This is considered extremely rude!

And as this is a time period where people died all the time for like, no reason (well actually there were lots of reasons, like for example 'not knowing what a bacteria is') – anyway the point is that several of these potential jesters don't like what you did, and let you know by pulling you back and shoving you into a handy pit filled with spikes.

In this version of reality, your body is dug up years down the line by this guy, Hamlet! He holds up your skull and looks at it and says "Alas, poor dude, but this is but one of the many Skulls here, for as you know in my father's tyme we did Shove rude people into the Pitte, and there they did Expire and in doing so finally learn their Lessonne."

Okay I know you're dead but I feel like I should tell you that I don't know why Hamlet's talking all fake old-timey either. It's 25 years in the FUTURE, Hamlet! We're not in olden times: history is the story of progress from less to more advanced! Geez!

Okay look, I've got to end your story here so I can talk to Hamlet about my personal theories of historiography. It's an emergency!

THE END

22 I – wow, okay, listen when I was all "Hey Yorick the fates totally want you dead today, just a heads up" I thought this would be a game of you deftly dodging death traps left and right, not one where you run as fast as you can into a stone wall marked "JOG INTO THIS HEAD-FIRST AT HIGH SPEED FOR FREE INSTA-DEATH".

But you're the boss!

You attack the king with your bare fists, and you manage one solid punch in the chest before you are set upon by the Royal Guards and the Royal Guards' Dogs, who tear you apart and feast on your flesh. The dogs do most of the feasting though.

You are buried in a shallow grave and 25 years later this guy Hamlet digs you up! He holds up your skull and examines it and says "Look at this scoring here, along the cranial ridge: it's characteristic of wolf or canine teeth. This man was eaten by either by dogs, by wolves . . . or by werewolves, I guess? BECAUSE THE WEREWOLF INVASION IS THE NEW THING THAT IS ROTTEN IN THE STATE OF DENMARK."

THE END

P.S. Oh I forgot to say: in this timeline, werewolves became real!! Everything's so nuts!

23 "The anecdote I am about to share with you comes from my time as a traveller," you say, "now many years behind me, I'm afraid! I had been questing with friends, and we had chance to approach the border between fair Denmark and Germany. Worried as I was that the border guards would accost us, I was heard to remark 'I certainly hope they don't think me to be an international murder person!'"

You pause, taking in the room. They seem – kinda interested in where this story is going? I guess?

"My travelling companions asked me with great sincerity what precisely I meant by that, and by my explanation it soon became clear that I had somehow forgotten the word 'assassin' and had been forced to invent a phrase to fill out that temporary gap in my personal lexicon."

You pause for laughter, but none comes. Someone coughs, which actually is the first recorded instance of this cliché ever actually happening in real life, so good work on that.

"That was a boring story, mommy!" Kid Hamlet says. "It's so boring I could cry," and then he actually starts to sob. What a jerk!

"Well, that was terrible," says King Hamlet. "I normally don't put people to death for being bad entertainers, but" and you don't catch the rest of it because a giant tree trunk on ropes has careened down from its hidden perch up in the rafters and slams into you sideways, mashing you against the far wall.

Your smushed-up bod is buried in a shallow grave, and 25 years later you're dug up by Kid Hamlet, now all grown up and going by 'Adult Hamlet', or 'Hamlet' for short! He picks up a fragment of your skull and seems to contemplate it, showing it to his friend Horatio.

"Alas, poor Yorick!" he says. "I knew him briefly, Horatio; a fellow of infinitely small jest, of most non-excellent fancy; he hath been borne into the wall by my dad's secret battering ram for being bad at japes." He tosses the fragment back into the grave.

"Isn't it weird to think about that?" replies Horatio. "Like, we all die sometime, you know? And then we just . . . decay. It's freaky to think of how biological we all are."

"Yeah man, bodies are gross. Never get one," says Hamlet, and then throws some dirt on top of your earthly remains and gets on with his business.

What business? Well I don't want to spoil anything but it involves a little thing called REGICIDE??

Hah hah, I'm just kidding, in this timeline it actually involves a little thing called GETTING ICE CREAM WITH FRIENDS?? That's right: the future's great, Yorick! Pals get ice cream all the time and also stop by graveyards on the way to dig up bodies for fun!

I'm really sorry you're missing out on it!!

THE END

24 Alone with Kid Hamlet, you make some more fart noises, and he continues to cheer. After about half an hour of this your lips are going a little numb, so you say "Listen, kid, what if I took a break for a whi–"

Kid Hamlet interrupts you and explains that your relationship is based on toot noises, NOT on human conversation. He does not want to hear another morpheme from you for the rest of your days, and the only phoneme he wants to hear is "thppppth". Kids say the craziest things, huh? And kid princes say the craziest things that instantly become law that is punishable by death!

So, you never say another word to Hamlet, but spend the rest of your life making toots both artificial and genuine, and making quite a comfortable living by doing so. Nicely done! In a time where most people have to personally kill a chicken if they want a chicken burger for lunch, you're living pretty comfortably. You die of a heart attack five years later (effective medicine is not a thing yet, heads up) and get buried in a shallow grave. A couple of decades later, Hamlet digs up your body! He picks up your skull and finds it remarkable, and therefore remarks upon it:

"Alas, poor Yorick!" he says. "I heard him toot, Horatio; a fellow of infinite toots, of most excellent toots; he hath tooted on me a thousand times. Yet where be his toots now? His super toots? His ultra toots extreme? His flashes of gas, that were wont to clear the table of its occupants because of the stank??"

I'll say this: of all the legacies it is possible to have, Yorick, this is certainly one of them.

THE END

25 Hamlet gasps. "That's terrible!" he says.

"I hate it!" he shouts, stomping his feet.

"I hate you!" he continues.

"Daddyyyyyyyyyyy!" he screams, running out of the room, in tears, his hands in the air. Geez but that kid sure feels things real deeply, huh? Anyway you try to leave but guards prevent you, and then the king shows up and makes apologetic noises about what he has to do now, but you understand the importance of family don't you Yorick, you know how children can be, hah hah hah, anyway you understand that I promised the child I'd do this for him, I just can't say no to him when he gets into one of these moods, hah hah hah.

Your skull is dug up twenty-five years later by none other than Hamlet: he's an adult now and in this timeline he works as a gravedigger! But in a profession seemingly populated entirely by wags and loveable rogues, he alone takes his job very seriously, so he disposes of your remains efficiently and without comment.

THE END

26 On your way out of the room, you bump into King Hamlet, who was coming to check in on you.

"Hey, I was just going to check in on you," he says, clearly unaware of my excellent and efficient narration. "How are things with Hamlet?"

"He . . . wants to ride me like a horse?" you say.

"I see. And why aren't you in there doing that right now, which is what I pay you for?"

"Because . . . I think . . . that sounds . . . um, sucky?" you say. It sounded better in your head. Honestly, Yorick, I think the problem was your delivery: those ellipses aren't doing you any favours. You should've done something like this:

"BECAUSE I THINK THAT SOUNDS SUCKY," you say.

Or even better:

"BECAUSE I THINK THAT SOUNDS SUCKY," you say, ripping open your shirt to reveal your rad chest hair that ruffles slightly in a passing breeze.

See what I did there? Drop the "um", ditch the pauses, and speak in all caps: THAT'S the way to command authority! Write that down, Yorick. Also work on your chest hair, Yorick.

Anyway you get fired and die a few days later from starvation (that apple only got you so far, bro!). You're buried in a shallow grave and your body is dug up 25 years later by Hamlet who, in this timeline, works as a scientist/inventor guy! He holds your skull in his hand and examines it closely.

"I simply cannot determine to whom this skull belonged beyond a reasonable doubt," he says.

THE END

27 Well great, because it is! But I like you, so I'll tell you what happens next: you're buried in a shallow grave and years later your skull is dug up by a street-wise and wise-cracking gravedigger! And by amazing coincidence, Hamlet himself is present at this exhumation, too. Here's what he says, and I'll annotate it for you so nobody gets lost:

"Alas, poor Yorick! I knew him, Horatio [that's his friend, he's there too, I should've mentioned that]; a fellow of infinite jest [he's talking about you now], of most excellent fancy [nice!]; he hath borne me on his back a thousand times [haha yeah you sure did]; and now, how abhorred in my imagination it is! My gorge rises at it [he's saying your body looks gross now]. Here hung those lips that I have kissed I know not how oft [wait, what? What? When did this happen]. Where be your gibes now? Your gambols? [Hey that reminds me, you never looked up what those were!] Your songs? Your flashes of merriment, that were wont to set the table on a roar? [he means you were a fun guest at dinner parties]"

Man, not bad eh? You made a really positive impact on this young man. And Hamlet turned out pretty okay, too! You know, I like the way this ending is going. Maybe I'll write a whole sequel to your little adventure, taking place in the future and starring adult Hamlet! Oh man, and he could have this whole super dramatic motivation and intense backstory, but secretly it's all just there to get us to this one callback in the graveyard scene! I'll call it *Yorick The Wacky Dude Who Gets His Head Dug Up Near The End, And Hamlet's In It Too!*.

Maybe I could shorten the title somehow?

Anyway, you should totally check this book out. I might even throw in a spooky ghost!!

THE END

28 You spend the next few months reading every book you can get your hands on about sharks. "A well-informed punch is a good punch," you say, hoping that this saying will catch on as well as "to thine own self be true" did. It doesn't, but that doesn't stop you from reading about sharks!

You learn a bunch of things. You learn that sharks have been around for millions of years and you think: amazing! You learn that humans are more likely to be killed by bees or dogs than sharks and you realize you always suspected those bees were up to something. And you learn sharks have sensitive gills and realize that that's definitely where you'll punch 'em.

Sharks are awesome. And now that you've done your research, you've realized one thing. You leave the library, raise your fists in the air, and shout your revelation to the heavens, and that revelation is:

• "I don't want to punch sharks! I want to help them!" Turn to 29
• "I definitely want to punch a shark, one of the gentle and loving kittens of the sea!" Turn to 42

29 You don't want to punch sharks. You want to help them! Their major predator is humans, who kill them out of fear, or so they can gobble their fins in a soup! You've spent your entire life wanting to punch a shark, but now you realize that all of this was wasted time.

You're not William SHARKSpeare. You never were! You're William Shakespeare, and you're gonna go out there and write yourself some plays. New and better plays, that inform the entire world that sharks are great and everyone should love them!

You're midway though composing your first one (*Antony and Cleopatra and A Cool Nice Shark*) when you step out for a drink with your friends Ben Jonson and Jon Ward. Unfortunately, while you're out, you contract a fever, and living as you do in an age before antibiotics, it kills you a few days later.

• Whoops: Turn to 30

30   You're dreaming in bed when death arrives.

You dream of meeting a shark, an impossible shark, one that can walk on land and breathe the air as you do. You apologize to the shark, saying you never meant to hurt her kind. The shark explains that's nice to hear, but apologizing to a single member of her species isn't really going to change anything. You laugh, and promise to do better. You spend more and more time with the shark. You fall in love.

Your lungs are failing now.

You and the shark are married in a wonderful ceremony, and it's perfect, so perfect, and before soon your children come, shark/human hybrids, as beautiful as any sight ever seen on this earth. They're perfect. Your life is perfect.

Your heart, at last, finds rest.

The children grow up, facing prejudice, sure, but also seeing the world in a way nobody ever could before. Their shared human/shark heritage brings them a perspective the planet sorely needs. You and your shark partner fight fiercely for them everywhere you go. Your life is filled up with love.

And as your brain slowly starves from a lack of oxygen, the dream takes on a new reality. Things seem to speed up. Your children graduate school, become the people they were always destined to be. You and your shark wife grow old and fat and happy.

One day your children come to visit you, now with children of their own. They tell you they'll be okay. They tell you it's fine if you need to leave. They tell you that you made a difference in not just their lives, but in the lives of the untold generations yet to come, shark/human hybrids that will live and love and laugh because of the choices you made over the course of your life. They gesture to your library, filled up with copies of your books, immortal, timeless books translated into every living language, and they tell you you'll never be forgotten. William Shakespeare, as you look over your legacy, you smile.

And then you die.

THE END

P.S. As you lie dying, your oxygen-starved mind whispers "Forsooth! Shark/human hybrids", and it's probably for the best that your real-life wife Anne never figured out why those were your last words because oh my gosh she would be SUPER PISSED.

31 The sharks are huge, with mouths full of teeth. These truly are the apex predators of the sea.

As you examine their savage beauty, you are overtaken by the desire to bop one real hard. You strip down to your underwear, dive into the ocean, swim up to the shark, and, completely unprovoked, punch it right in the . . .

• eye, with a full-strength Widowmaker Express punch: **Turn to 49**
• nose, with a medium-strength "my arms are windmills and I'm slowly swimming towards you" array of punches: **Turn to 50**
• gills, with a gentle love tap: **Turn to 51**

32 Shakespeare, what are you doing?! Sharks have evolved to eat thrashing animals in the water, especially wounded ones, and you're paddling around covered in blood!

You instantly attract a whole bunch of other sharks, the first of which bites off your punchin' hand, and the second of which bites off your everything else.

This, it turns out, is super fatal.

THE END

33 "I don't care," the jester says, pressing the sword in harder against your throat, "Give me more money or I kill you."

Maybe it was what you said? A properly-chosen quotation from your own work might impress this jester a bit more!

• Grit your teeth and say "A man can die but once (*Henry IV*: *Part 2*, Act 3, Scene 2)" **Turn to 53**
• Grit your teeth and say "Cowards die many times before their deaths;

the valiant never taste of death but once (*Julius Caesar*, Act 2, Scene 2)"
Turn to 53
• Smile and say "The better part of valour is discretion (*Henry IV: Part 1*, Act 5, Scene 4)" **Turn to 52**

34 You open the book and read the following words:

It's a brand new day! You roll over in bed, open your eyes and, as you do every day, remind yourself of who and where you are, as well as what your deal is.

"I live in Denmark," you whisper to the ceiling. "And my name is Yorick. I'm a man of infinite jest and most excellent fancy."

"That means I'm good at jokes and have a cool imagination," you remind yourself. "But that don't pay the bills. I'm broke, there's nothing for breakfast, and if I don't find a job today so I can pay for some food I WILL LITERALLY DIE."

Oh! Before we get started here, Yorick, I should probably mention that your life has the potential to have an improbably large effect on the future. The good news is that you're a temporal hinge upon which all our tomorrows rest! The bad news is that the only way for you to put this legacy into motion is by dying. But the good news part two is that it's really really really really insanely likely that you're gonna die today!

Okay!

Have fun!!

• Get out of bed and go for a walk: **Turn to 35**
• Stay in bed: **Turn to 54**
• Die instantly, I want my legacy to begin NOW: **Turn to 20**

You roll out of bed, put in your walkin' shoes (if we're being honest they're the only pair you own, so they're also your runnin' shoes and holes-in-'em shoes but that's neither here nor there) and walk out into the crisp morning air. As you stroll around your small village you notice a sign nailed to a tree! You think "look sign" to yourself, and this is what you see:

"Wow!" you say out loud. "All my problems of not having cash would be solved if I got paid cash money!!" Then you tear the ad down so you can take it with you (also this prevents other people from applying for the job; Yorick, you are a young man whose fancy sometimes lightly turns to lawless self-interest.)

You decide to make your way down to the royal court to totally get this job. When you get there at 1:50 pm, you see several other potential jesters have arrived at well!

• Sabotage the other jesters: Turn to 56
• Await your turn: Turn to 36
• Push your way to the front of the line: Turn to 21

36 You patiently await your turn. While you wait, you start to chat with the jester next to you. He's wearing red leotards printed with white diamonds, and has face paint on that exaggerates his features. He explains to you that Jesters have a long and proud tradition. They fall into two camps: the "natural fool", or someone who really is a big dummy, and the "licensed fool", who is given permission to just act like a big dummy. Licensed fools tend to last longer, because natural fools don't know when to keep their mouths shut. "The jester is a special job," he says, "We're entertainers, sure, but we're also able to directly address the regent in a way few others can. That is the special magic of the jest."

"To be a jester," he intones with great gravity, "is both an honour and a privilege."

"What's your act?" you ask.

"I put a squirrel in my pants and then act real upset that there is a squirrel in my pants," he says.

King Carl Hamlet sticks his head into the room and looks around. He points to you and says "You're up, chuckles!"

• Enter the Royal Court: Turn to 37
• Push your new friend forward instead: Turn to 57
• Attack the king: Turn to 22

37 You shyly step into the Royal Court. It's a beautiful room, clearly capable of entertaining the entire monarchy of this here country (Denmark, in case you forgot). But right now it's mostly empty. The only people here are your king (Carl Hamlet, who's walking ahead of you, intent on settling into his throne), your queen (Gertrude Hamlet, smiling politely), and their son, Hamlet Jr. He looks to be about five years old.

"Pleased to meet you, your majesties," you say. "I am Yorick."

"This is our son, Kid Hamlet," says the king. "He's getting to be a bit of a handful as he grows up, and we want to keep him entertained. Since nobody has yet invented an automatic entertainment system – perhaps where automatons and mechanical men perform plays at our merest whim and we can pause them should we desire to get up to for a drink, or 'rewind' them should we miss something and wish to revisit it – as I say, since this as not yet been invented, we have to reply on actual alive people to entertain us."

" . . . Okay," you say. "Um, I'm an alive person. I can do that."

"Wonderful!" says the king. "Please, proceed."

• Recount a charming jape: **Turn to 23**
• Make a fart noise by blowing between your hands, and then look around accusingly and say "Whoah, that wasn't me" **Turn to 38**
• Make a pass at the Queen: **Turn to 59**

38 You do that thing. The king and queen look unimpressed, but Kid Hamlet loves it. He cheers and claps and launches into a long soliloquy on how great it was. When he's done, the king says "Well, I didn't think that was super rad, but my kid loved it and your job is to entertain him, so good job! You're hired . . . um, what did you say your name was again?"

"Yorick, sir" you say. "It's either a corruption of the Scandinavian 'Erick' or 'Jorg', but it might also be an anagram of the Greek 'kurios', which–"

King Hamlet cuts you off. "Okay, cool, I'm not super into hearing more.

I'm going to leave you alone with Kid Hamlet: if you can survive the day, I'll pay you a bunch of gold and let you live in the castle. Deal?"

"Deal," you say, stepping forward and to shake his outstretched hand. While you're doing that you say, "Oh hey, can I have some food? I'm literally starving."

"Sure!" says the king, and pulls an apple out from inside his robes, tossing it to you. "Kick ass," you say, swallowing the apple whole. Hey! How'd you do that? That was awesome! I want to be able to do that too.

In any case, you are no longer in immediate danger of dying! From starvation, I mean!

• Talk to Kid Hamlet: Turn to 39
• Make more fart noises: Turn to 24
• Beg the king not to leave you alone with Kid Hamlet: Turn to 60

39 "Hey kid, I'm glad you liked my toot noises," you say when you're left alone with him. "What else do you like?"

"PLENTLY," says Hamlet in that squeaky voice little kids have that's adorable for at least . . . a little while? "I like include gibes, gambols, songs, AND flashes of merriment."

"I can do those," you say, making a mental note to look up what gibes and gambols are. They sound like body parts, maybe. Maybe they're special parts on, like, the inside of a fish?

"I also like riding you like a horse and will require that you carry me on your back at least one thousand times."

"Um, okay," you say, offering what you hope is a confident smile.

"Per year," says Hamlet.

• Say "Right." and get down on all fours: Turn to 40
• Say "Hah! Nice try, kid. I'm not that poor!" and leave the room: Turn to 26

40   Kid Hamlet jumps onto your back (ouch!) and slaps you on the back of the head. "Yip yip!" he shouts.

I guess that means go? You gallop around the room on your hands and knees, which is super painful because the floor is literally made of rock, but get a brief reprieve when you hear a cough. You turn around and see King Hamlet, leaning against a doorframe and smiling.

"Everything's going great in here then, huh?" he says.

"Yep!" you say confidently. "This is exactly where I wanted my career to bring me!"

"Super," says the king, and leaves. Kid Hamlet jumps down from your back and stands in front of you. He looks very serious. It's kind of adorable.

"I want you to give me a nickname," he says, "and if you choose a bad one, then I'm going to ask daddy to kill you, and he'll do it because he loves me."

You blink.

"Now!" he says.

- Nickname him "The Hammer" Turn to 41
- Nickname him "Li'l Hamster" Turn to 61
- Nickname him "Porkchop Weebottoms" Turn to 25

41   "I love it!" he says. "Hammers are tough, like me, but also decisive, like me!"

"Phew," you say.

"Yay! Phew!!" he repeats, running around the room. "The Hammer! The Hammer!"

He punches you in the head.

"The Hammer!!" he says.

"Ow," you say.

Anyway, you get Hamlet to calm down: you sing and dance and tell stories and make fun of your own smile and before you know it you even start to . . . like your job? Yes. You like your job. You like that each morning you have the laughter of a child to look forward to as a reward for a job well done.

Also, they pay you!

A few weeks go by. You pour a flagon of Rhenish wine on a young gravedigger's head. Hamlet loves it. Those weeks turn into months, and before you know it, years. Everything is great, and Kid Hamlet changes before your eyes into Young Adult Hamlet, and then Teen Hamlet. You scale up your stories to match. And then you die of a heart attack.

THE END

• Accept that this is the end: Turn to 27
• Refuse to accept that this is the end: Turn to 62

42 You charter a ship to go look for sharks to punch. You feel guilty about doing it, now that you know how great sharks are, but it's been your lifelong dream and you're not about to stop now.

Luckily for you, fate intervenes! You're not on your ship for more than a few days when it's rammed by a colossal shark. Let me tell you about this shark, Shakespeare. It's enormous. It's powerful. And it's completely insane. It dove down too deep and got ocean madness! It hates all other life, and if you don't stop it now, it won't rest until it's taken a bite out of every single thing in the ocean. And honestly, it sounds impossible, but I'm not even certain it'll stop there. It may try to kill everything on land, and then the skies, and eventually space too. This insane megashark needs to be stopped, if life on Earth is to survive.

In other words, this insane megashark needs to be punched . . .

. . . RIGHT IN THE FRIGGIN' GILLHOLE.

You feel your punchin' arm twitch in anticipation.

• Finally! Justification! I can now feel really good about punching this shark!! **Turn to 43**

43 Your good feelings are interrupted as the ferocious beast leaps out of the water towards you, smashing into your ship at top speed. Not just into it – THROUGH it. The shark bursts through one side of the hull and out the other, and you're so stunned at what you just saw that it takes you a second to realize that water is now rushing into your vessel.

This ship, Shakespeare, is going down.

You run towards the lifeboats. The captain is there, directing everyone to safely. When she sees you she points you towards a particular boat with nobody else in it and yells at you to get into that one.

"It's the one for guests!" she says. "My crew and I will take the other, sturdier boats!"

"Wait, what?" you say, momentarily stripped of your normal Shakespearean eloquence. But there's no time: she shoves you into the lifeboat, drops you into the water, and leaps into her own lifeboat just before the entire ship sinks beneath the waves.

You're slightly miffed that you got the sucky lifeboat when the shark returns, swimming up from the depths of the ocean at top speed. It leaps into the air from the water (like a dolphin, you think), pirouettes in mid-air (like a ballerina, you think), and descends towards the other lifeboats head-first, mouth open (like a terrifying nightmare from the unknowable depths of the ocean that no human eye was ever meant to see, you think). The captain and her crew are gobbled in a single bite. You're the last one left.

You look down and see the shark turning around for another pass. It's shooting up from the water . . . right at you.

• THIS IS IT! Wind up for a punch! **Turn to 44**
• THIS IS IT! Wind up for a hug!! **Turn to 63**

44 You pull back your arm.

You curl your fingers into a fist.

You imagine dramatic music swelling.

The shark leaps from the water, right in front of your lifeboat. This is your moment, one that you'll always remember, especially because we painted it on the front of this book. You put your full weight into it . . .

. . . and you punch.

• KA-POW! Turn to 45

45 It's the greatest punch of your life, Shakespeare. Your punch deflects the shark backwards, and it bellyflops into the sea, taking 10 damage. That's great!

The bad news is the shark still has 1490 damage left. And it's swimming back for another attack!

• Punch it again: Turn to 46
• Hug it this time: Turn to 55

46 It's the second-greatest punch of your life, Shakespeare. Your punch deflects the shark backwards, and it bellyflops into the sea, taking 9 damage. That's not bad at all!

The bad news is the shark still has 1481 damage left. And it's swimming back for another attack!

• Punch it again: Turn to 47
• Hug it this time: Turn to 55

47 It's the tenth-greatest punch of your life, Shakespeare. Your punch barely deflects the shark backwards, and it bellyflops into the sea, taking a mere 1 damage.

This is definitely going to take a while.

The bad news is the shark still has 1480 damage left. And it's swimming back for another attack!

- Punch it again! PUNCH IT AGAIN: Turn to 48
- Hug it this time: Turn to 55

48 This time your punches level up, and at the same time, you get a critical hit! YES! You KNEW something like this would have to happen eventually!

The shark takes 45,000 damage and explodes. You are covered in shark guts.

You are also covered in some human guts too, since the shark just ate a bunch of humans.

- Clean off by swimming in the sea: Turn to 32
- Stay in lifeboat, paddle towards shore: Turn to 64

49 You wind up your patented Widowmaker and punch the shark, completely unprovoked, right in the eye.

KABLAM!

You're so happy at having achieved both of your two life goals (write good, punch sharks) that it barely makes a dent in your mood when you notice how the shark is understandably enraged and comes right at you with its powerful jaws wide open.

- Aw geez: Turn to 67

50 You announce that your arms are windmills (waterwheels would've made more sense, Shakespeare, but you're used to doing this on land, so I'll excuse it), and explain that you can't control them. They go around and around punching and punching, and there's nothing you can do to stop the punches as you swim up towards the shark. And then . . .

BAM! BAM! BAM! BAM!

You punch the shark over and over, completely unprovoked, right in the eye. William Shakespeare, you have punched a shark! You have achieved your life's goals, which is something that not everyone gets to say – but you get to say it, right now. You did exactly what you said you would do: you wrote some amazing words, and you punched a friggin' shark.

You're basking in your glory when an understandably enraged shark swims at you at top speed, its powerful jaws wide open.

• Aw geez: Turn to 67

51 You tap the shark right in the gills playfully, in the way a friend might gently punch another friend on the shoulder at a garden party while saying "Oh Shakespeare! Your odd obsessions will be the death of you, I swear!" The shark is understandably upset at this contact, but shark gills are actually sensitive parts, and it swims away from you to avoid getting touched there again. This shark doesn't want any trouble.

That still counts though! Congratulations, Shakespeare: you have successfully punched a shark, which all true historians agree was really important to you. Your life's goals are now complete.

So . . . now what?

• Punch another shark!! I wrote more than one play, I'm gonna punch more than one shark! Turn to 67
• Swim back to boat: Turn to 65

52 "Does that mean you're going to give me more money?" the jester asks.

"No," you say, "you've got it all. But, um, I'll write you a poem. That's got value! You'll get your own poem by William Shakespeare, all about you. How's about that? You'll let me live for that, right?"

The jester squints at you, suspicious. "Maybe. What rhyming scheme are we talkin' about here?" he asks.

"ABAB CDCD EE." you say.

"TWO quatrains and a rhyming couplet?" he says, excited. "Mister, you've got yourself a deal!" He releases the blade from your neck, and you take a few paces back, rubbing the skin where the blade was.

"Well?" he says.

You clear your throat and begin your poem.

• I think that I shall never see . . . **Turn to 69**
• My name is Shakespeare and I'm here to say . . . **Turn to 68**
• Roses are red . . . **Turn to 70**

53 "Is that a threat?" the jester says. "Are you threatening me with that 'die but once' stuff?"

"I – Maybe?" you say.

"Well, here's your one taste of death." The jester says, and stabs you. It's really gross so I won't describe it here, but suffice it to say that he stabs you through some VERY important organs.

And that, gentle reader, is how come Shakespeare never wrote any more plays! He died in the woods quoting himself to a stranger.

54 Hah hah, weren't you listening to yourself earlier? You're starving and you need to get a job. But I guess you figured that's a problem for Future Yorick to deal with, because Present Yorick has decided to stay in bed. While in bed, you, Present Yorick:

– sigh and stare at the ceiling
– grab your sketchbook and draw what you and your friends would look like if you were all cats
– listen to birds and imagine what it would be like if you could talk to birds
– die

Oh well, Yorick! Your body is buried in a shallow grave and lies undisturbed for twenty-five years, at which point it's dug up by this guy, Hamlet, who holds up your skull and says:

"Alas, poor dead guy! I did not know him, Horatio; but judging by the shape of his skull and other phrenological features he was a fellow of infinite willfulness, furthermore the parts of the skull associated with secretiveness and philoprogenitiveness are pronounced, which to me suggests he was likely a member of the criminal class, perhaps a Kingpin or other Crime Admiral."

What the – that doesn't describe you at all! You are about to protest this until you remember you're dead and your flesh already got gobbled by worms! Circle of life, Yorick!

THE END

55 Your arms wrap around the rough skin of the shark, and you quickly find out that hugging a shark that's leaping out of the water means you get carried out of the water with the shark too. You look down as the ocean falls away beneath you, experience a brief moment of weightlessness at the peak of your flight, and then fall back down towards the water.

"I was born in the sea," you shout, referencing a fact that could at least maybe be true and in any case can't be disproven by evidence available to scholars today, "and to the sea I shall return!!"

The shark says nothing in response.

You slam into the ocean, still hugging the shark tight. Water fills your lungs, but still you don't let go. "This is my legend," you think to yourself. "People will read the words of Shakespeare for generations, true, but what will live on for even longer is the legend of how I was obsessed with punching sharks my entire life, went to sea in order to punch a shark, and instead, hugged that shark and then drowned."

"Wait," you think, "that's not actually that compelling a legen–" but I'm sorry to say that in that moment cracks a noble heart, and you drown.

Goodnight, sweet Shakespeare, and schools of fish sing thee to thy rest!

THE END

P.S. I know that it was technically only one fish that sung thee to thy rest, and it was more of a "attack dive" than a song, but come on, I'm making the most of what you gave me here, Shakespeare.

56 You decide that the best way to get this job is not to earn it by being the best candidate, but rather get it by ensuring nobody else is a viable candidate. In a single word of French origin: sabotage!

You ponder for a bit on the subject of moral universalism (if an act is just, then it's just for everyone to perform the act) and you imagine a universe in which everyone sabotages everyone else to get ahead. It seems terrible! So you conclude the only way to get ahead in such a universe is to sabotage everybody else first, and in doing so transform the Golden Rule ("Do unto others as you would have them do unto you") into the Iron Rule ("Do unto others before they can do unto you first"). 'The Iron Rule' sounds more badass so you're big into it!

Your first sabotage attempt is to pull down the pants of one of the other jesters, but he notices when you do that and stabs you right through the brains.

Your body finds its way into a shallow grave, and 25 years later it's dug up by Hamlet! He picks up your skull and says "Whoah, check it out! The knife this guy got stabbed with is still here, and you can see how it went right through his eye and then popped out on the back of his skull! BAD. ASS."

Hamlet adds the knife to his inventory and returns your skull to its grave. "I can use this knife in the future to open many things, such as for example a sealed letter or perhaps a jammed window," he says.

Remember when I said you'd have an effect on the future? Well, that was it. You eventually help a thirty-year-old graverobber open a jammed window, by being the skull he stole an old knife from.

BEHOLD YOUR LEGACY, YORICK.

THE END

57 "Take this guy instead!" you say, shoving your new friend forward. "Look, he's even wearing special pants. Aren't they festive?"

"I guess," says the king. "Okay, pants guy – come in and show me what you've got!"

That was a really nice thing to do, Yorick! Unfortunately it doesn't work out for you because your new friend gets the job you wanted and as he's leaving you say "Hey, can I have some money for food so I don't die?" and he looks at you derisively and says "What do you take me for, a natural fool?" and kicks you in the chest knocking you over and man that was impolite and not at all called for! Also you hit your head on the tile floor and die (sorry!) (but I did warn you how fate had it in for you today, sooooo).

"That was a dick move, New Jester!" says the king. "I will not have casual acts of murder committed in this castle, for the only way that will end is with literally everyone killing everyone else, and I for one sure would hate to ever see a story end that way. Okay, off with his head!"

You're buried in a shallow grave with your murderer. 25 years later Hamlet digs you up and picks up your skull and says "Alas, poor – wait, there's another dude in here too? Aw man, sick!"

Hamlet picks up the other skull and now, with one skull per hand, puts on a skull puppet show. He has you dance around and crack wise, and he even makes you kiss, which he simulates by knocking the two skulls together again and again. It's not the most respectful thing in the world?

Huh! I bet this is why most stories end when the main character dies and don't continue to show in gruesome detail what happened to their bones decades down the road when they're dug up by a stranger, right?

"Writing." What do I know?

THE END

58 You rush out on the first ship you can find, which it turns out is on an oceanic sailing ship. The only way on board is to enlist as a hired hand, so that's what you do. It's hard work, but it makes your muscles look awesome, and you are excited to return to England because when you do you'll be both the greatest AND most ripped author of all time!

One day, out at see, you spot a school of sharks.

• Finally! My well-established shark-punching obsession can reach its climax! EXAMINE SHARKS: Turn to 31
• Naw. Return to England, super ripped, and write more plays! Turn to 16

59 "Before I start," you say, "may I just ask one question?"

"Sure," says the king.

You make eye contact with Gertrude and raise an eyebrow, in a manner you hope is suggestive. "I guess I was just wondering how the queen got to be so hot??" you say.

"Did it like – happen as you . . . got older?" you continue.

"Aw man," says the king, raising a hand to stop you. "I don't mind people making passes at the Queen, but I do mind when they're so incredibly terrible. I'm afraid your story ends here, Yorick."

You're put to death (ouch!) and buried in a shallow grave. Some decades later you're dug up by Kid Hamlet, who's all grown up now and who has dropped the diminutive, so he's just "Ham" now. Yep. "Prince Ham" is his name. Look, we don't all make great decisions all the time, just keep that in mind before you make fun, okay?

Prince Ham holds up your skull and says "For some reason this guy reminds me of a man I knew for only a few minutes twenty-five years ago."

He's talking about you, Yorick!!

"If I remember correctly, and I believe I do, he made a real sucky pass at my mom," Ham says, tossing your skull back into the grave. And that, my friend, is the very last time anyone ever remembers you, thinks about your life, or says your name for the absolute rest of eternity.

THE END

P.S. Oh! Excluding this book, of course!

60 "Um – did you have to leave so soon?" you say.

" . . . Yes?" says the king. "I am the head of state here. I've got a whole country to run."

"Please don't leave me alone with this tiny human that you and your wife boinked into existence," you say, getting down on your knees. The fact that you're asking this in the first place is weird, but man your phrasing didn't help matters! "Boinked?"

"Boinked?" says the king.

"It refers to sexual congress," you say.

"Oh," says the King. "Gross. Okay, anyway, you're dead now," and one of the advantages of kings is they get to make declarative sentences like that while having the full resources of a nation to ensure that those statements come true!

So you get killed (dude chops off your head, bam) and your body gets buried in a shallow pile of other bodies. 25 years later Hamlet comes across your skull and says "Alas, poor Yorick, he taught me what 'boinked' means. At great personal cost too, if I remember correctly. Hah hah, weird."

That afternoon Hamlet successfully deploys 'boinked' in a sentence, and that is your legacy, my friend! And your final score is . . . 'boinked out of ten'? That's not very good!!

THE END

61 "I AM NOT A CREPUSCULAR RODENT" he shouts, tears in his eyes, while nevertheless adorably stumbling over the pronunciation of "crepuscular". You're impressed that this kid knows a word meaning "active primarily during dawn and dusk" and further impressed at how I worked the definition so seamlessly into the story, so even if you didn't know what the word meant, that's not a problem now!

Anyway Li'l Hamster's as good as his word, and the king ends your tenure as an alive human. Your tenure as a decaying body beings at once and proceeds uneventfully for 25 years until Li'l Hamster himself digs up your skull!

"Alas and dangs, Horatio! This is the guy who gave me that terrible nickname I hate!" he says, examining your skull in his hand. "It's because of him that I had to leave the royal court and start a new life as a gravedigger."

"I am familiar with your origin story," replies Horatio.

"Hmph." says Li'l Hamster, and throws your skull into a pile of other skulls for him to take home later. He collects them! This timeline is really weird!!

Your final score is "man why'd you have to make it weird" out of a hundred!

What? Not allowed. This IS the end, you just died of a heart att–

–wait, it says here you . . . got better? It says you stood up and said "My heart fixed itself guys, neat" and then . . . went about your business?

FOR TWENTY-FIVE YEARS??

So now it's twenty-five years in the future and you're standing beside your friend Hamlet and your mutual friend Horatio. You're in the middle of one of your madcap adventures you guys always get into together, which has led you to a graveyard. A gravedigger is digging into a shallow grave. Well good luck, Yorick, because I know he's about to dig up your skull and then you're gonna be in trouble. Here it comes! Right now!!

 . . . The gravedigger continues digging without incident.

Hamlet seems like he's about to say something, and gets as far as "Alas, poor . . . Yor–I, um. Wh–" and then there's this terrible light bursting out of his chest, tearing him apart. What happens next happens over the course of just a few microseconds, but I'll slow it down so you know what happens:

The light bursts out of Hamlet, blinding everyone who sees it, including you. It grows, splitting apart the very fabric of reality as it goes, tearing down through the graveyard and up into the sky. The Earth itself is blasts apart in two colossal fragments – and you'd think that would be the end of it, but no: your li'l tear in spacetime continues to expand, laterally now, until a few nanoseconds later it contains the entire planet. Or it would, if the planet still existed, which it doesn't. Erased from existence, bucko. You destroyed all our tomorrows with your paradox, and 2 million years later this quadrant of the universe is avoided by every single spacefaring race because it's RUINED.

I told you earlier the universe required you to die! You were supposed to be buried here so Hamlet would have the chance reflect upon your skull, but yeah, tearing the universe a new one so you could steal an extra few years was so totally worth it.

Jerk!!

THE END FOR REAL,
THANKS FOR NOTHING

63 You spread your arms wide.

You splay out your fingers in a way you hope is friendly.

You imagine nice music swelling that you could easily hug to.

The shark leaps from the water, right in front of your lifeboat. This is your moment, one that you'll always remember, especially since even in a book that has a scene of you punching this very shark on the cover, you have chosen the path of nonviolence. You put your full weight into it . . .

. . . and you hug.

• Aww! Turn to 55

64 You paddle away from the gore and direct yourself towards shore. It takes 15 hours of paddling and you're exhausted at the end, but you make it back to port.

You're covered in gore, but you're safe, sound, and successful.

You've written the best plays of all time, and you've also punched the biggest shark of all time so hard THAT HE EXPLODED. You've not only lived your best life, Shakespeare, you've lived THE best life it's possible to live. You're the greatest person Earth has ever produced.

You feel like there's nothing you can't do. And it turns out – that's true! A partial list of the things you can now accomplish includes:

– climbing walls and crushing ice in your bare hands
– inspiring envy in others while also winning their lasting friendship
– ripping your shirt open by flexing your pectoral muscles
– saving babies from tornadoes
– jumping two buses (which you've invented) in a motorcycle (which you've also invented)
– travelling to the future and returning unscathed
– listening to the voice of God without exploding
– swimming up waterfalls

You accomplish all of those feats in rapid succession, and for the rest of time, people call you "The Bard of Avon": "bard", of course, being an acronym that stands for "Bad-Ass Radical Dude".

This is the best ending in the book, and by finding it, you, the reader, are officially as much a B.A.R.D. as Shakespeare ever was. In fact, you're in better shape! Shakespeare's feats were forgotten by history (some scholars don't believe the man could've done something as prosaic as write his own plays, so the parts of the historical record where he punched sharks and jumped over buses were excised as non-canon very early on), but in contrast, your feats all await you in the future. You've got nothing but potential. You can still be the greatest you there ever was.

Here is a certificate proclaiming that very message for you to cut out and frame! Congratulations; you've earned it!!

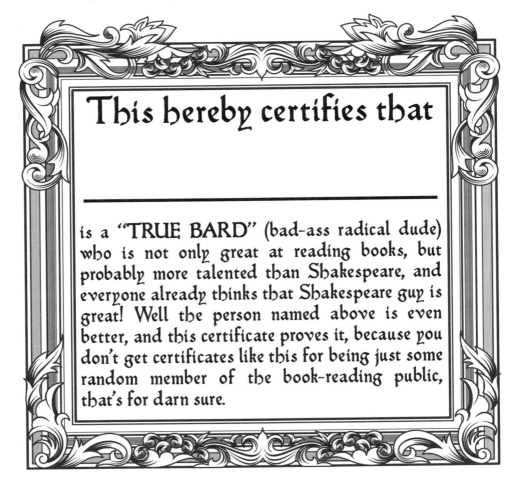

This hereby certifies that

_____

is a "TRUE BARD" (bad-ass radical dude) who is not only great at reading books, but probably more talented than Shakespeare, and everyone already thinks that Shakespeare guy is great! Well the person named above is even better, and this certificate proves it, because you don't get certificates like this for being just some random member of the book-reading public, that's for darn sure.

THE END

• Wait, wait, you said Shakespeare can travel through time now? THIS ISN'T THE END, MAKE SHAKESPEARE TRAVEL BACK IN TIME AND PUNCH A DINOSAUR! **Turn to 66**

65 The other sailors shout down that they don't want you around here anymore. Shakespeare, you're a hired hand who stripped down to his underwear and attacked a shark for no reason. The sailors don't need this trouble. They say they're a muscley and superstitious lot, and you just brought bad luck upon them all.

They refuse to let you back on board, and sail off without you. You're left treading water in a school of sharks.

Hours pass. You think the sailors might come back for you – this is all a prank, right? Some sort of hazing ritual? – but they haven't yet. You're getting tired. You can't swim forever. What do you do?

• Swim, try to find an island: **Turn to 71**
• Tread water some more, the sailors are definitely coming back: **Turn to 82**

66 You know what? You deserve it. A special ending, just for you:

You go back in time and punch a friggin' Utahraptor right on the nose. AND YOU SURVIVE THE EXPERIENCE.

THE END

P.S. By being bold enough to travel back in time and punch dinosaurs, you've unlocked a new game mode on this book! Simply re-read this story from the start, but every time you see "shark", mentally substitute the word "dinosaur". You'll be fighting a very unusual underwater dinosaur that breathes through gills, BUT BREATHING THROUGH GILLS ACTUALLY MAKES SENSE FOR AN UNDERWATER DINOSAUR, so there are absolutely no problems with this idea. Enjoy your new, a thousand times more awesome book, and thank you for reading!

P.P.S. You know, both this book, and in general.

P.P.P.S. It's really hard to compete with movies for the attention of a modern audience is the thing, so I appreciate your time here today.

67 The shark bites you and kills you, obviously. Nobody is surprised when this happens. You don't die instantly, mind you, but rather you die very slowly and painfully over the next few hours as you succumb to your shark bite. As you are dragged back to the boat by your rescuers, all baffled by your actions, you moan things like "why did I do that?" and "humans are a much greater threat to sharks than sharks are to humans", and "there have only been a handful of unprovoked attacks by sharks on humans in recorded history, unfortunately as I absolutely provoked this animal, this does not fall into that category."

You die, but your writing was famous enough that it lives on for hundreds and hundreds of years. In fact, your name becomes synonymous with "writing that's pretty good, but if we're being honest with each other how great can it really be if the state has to force you to read it by making it a mandatory part of the high school curriculum? Furthermore, as more modern authors can be inspired by, and in fact, fully rip off Shakespeare's work with impunity, isn't it possible that they could improve it, perhaps by adding space ships or laser beams? Actually, the more I think about it, the more seems crazy to think that a piece of work could be perfected hundreds and hundreds of years ago and not be improved, not even once, by the great mass of humanity that came afterwards."

THE END

PS. It's a long thing for your name to be synonymous with, but here we are!

68 "My name is Shakespeare and I'm here to say,
I'm into court jesters in a major way,
And if you don't like it that's okay,
Because handling disagreements civilly is foundational to any polite socie-tay"

The court jester stares at you in shock.

"THAT DIDN'T EVEN MATCH THE PROMISED ABAB RHYMING STRUCTURE!" he shouts, outraged, "AND THAT'S PUTTING ASIDE THE FORCED RHYME OF 'SOCIE-TAY!'"

• Get stabbed by the jester: Turn to 76

69 "I think that I shall never see
A jester as lovely as a tree
A tree whose hungry mouth is pressed
Against the earth's sweet flowing breast"

The court jester stares at you in shock.

"THAT'S AN AABB RHYMING STRUCTURE, PLUS ITS WAY TOO SIMPLE AND PREDICTABLE! ALSO IT DOESN'T EVEN SOUND LIKE SOMETHING YOU WROTE, AND IN MY OPINION THE REFERENCE TO FLOWING BREASTS SEEMED FORCED, AND I'M ADDITIONALLY 99% SURE IT'S PLAGIARIZED SOMEHOW" he shouts, outraged.

• Get stabbed by the jester: Turn to 76

70 "Roses are red," you say,
"Violets are blue,
After men are dead,
Lives the evil they do"

"Terrific!" exclaims the jester. "It matches the ABAB format required, and for some reason I feel this 'Roses are red' format could be used for all sorts of poems!" He paces in a small circle, composing his own knock-off poetry.

"Roses are red," he says, "violets are blue, I'm a 14 triple wide, for both my pants and my shoe." He laughs. "Roses are red, violets are blue, Shakespeare's writing for me, and if he stops he'll be through!"

Those are all ABCB, not ABAB! What the heck, jester? But given the circumstances, you decide not to correct him. Instead, you mutter "Roses are red, violets are blue, OMFG, STFU" – incidentally inventing both those acronyms on the spot. Hey. Nicely done, man.

"What was that?" he says.

"Nothing," you say. "I have your next verse ready."

• Are you going to Scarborough fair . . . **Turn to 74**
• Tyger tyger, burning bright . . . **Turn to 73**
• Whose woods these are, I think I know: **Turn to 72**

71 You pick a direction and start swimming. Just when you think you have nothing left to give, you spot a dot on the horizon, and it reenergizes you. Land!

Gasping, wheezing, you pull yourself ashore. Once you've recovered, you begin exploring. There's birds that live here, and coconuts: if you manage your resources well, you can survive.

But you can't escape.

Years pass, and you are still marooned on this island. You keep writing, new stories this time, like *A Midsummer Night's Morning After, The Taming Of Even More Shrews*, and *Julius Caesar Meets Macbeth, But They're Secretly Ghosts Trapped In Purgatory, And This Fact Is Revealed In The Third Act Twist*. I will say this, Shakespeare: living on an island with only birds to talk to has not improved your writing.

You die, and while your "lost works" are never found, the greatest scholars of the future will nevertheless be certain that you probably definitely ended up on a tropical island where you wrote new plays on giant leaves.

71

Back in England, your friends, embarrassed that you died trying to punch a shark, cover it up as best they can. They say you died "suddenly" and "too soon", and not because "the greatest mind in English literature had been inexplicably obsessed with punching a shark since his birth". They dig a grave, have a funeral, and lower a decoy coffin filled with rocks into the ground. Then they set up a gravestone, which is the reason why – very suspiciously, in retrospect – your epitaph, the epitaph of WILLIAM FRIGGIN' SHAKESPEARE, doesn't extoll your writing, mention your successes, or even remark upon all the lives you touched with your great work while you were alive. Instead, your gravestone spends 100% of its time telling everyone to definitely not try digging for Shakespeare here:

Good friend, for Jesus' sake forbear
To dig the dust enclosed here.
Blessed be the man that spares these stones,
And cursed be he that moves my bones.

Wake up, sheeple.

THE END

72 "Whose woods these are I think I know," you say.
"His house is in the village though;
He will not see me stopping here
To watch his woods fill up with snow."

The jester is extremely skeptical of your poem, and not just because it's summer and there's no snow anywhere.

"That poem . . . it really doesn't sound like you," he says. You get the distinct sense he wants to say something like "For some reason I have the strangest sense that it's plagiarized from someone I want to call 'Robert Frost' in the distant future?"

• Interrupt him before he can complete this thought: Turn to 84

73 "Tyger Tyger, burning bright," you say,
"In the forests of the night;
What immortal hand or eye,
Could frame thy fearful symmetry?"

The jester is extremely skeptical of your poem, and not just because you tried to rhyme "eye" with "symmetry".

"That poem . . . it really doesn't sound like you," he says. You get the distinct sense he wants to say something like "For some reason I have the strangest sense that it's plagiarized from someone I want to call 'William Blake' in the not-too-distant future?"

• Interrupt him before he can complete this thought: Turn to 84

74 "Are you going to Scarborough Fair?" you ask, rhetorically, as you recite your poem. "Parsley, sage, rosemary, and thyme / Remember me to one who lives there / She once was a true love of mine."

"That meets the CDCD rhyming scheme required," says the jester, satisfied for the moment.

"That's because I just composed it for you," you say, "right here on the spot. In fact, if I had to hazard a guess, I'd say that this poem will eventually become quite popular in the future, and while historians from that same future will only be able to trace the lyrics back to a Scottish poem called 'The Elfin Knight' dating from around 1670, none will ever realize that, I, William Shakespeare, definitely composed these rhymes while being held up in the woods by a down-on-his-luck court jester! That is, of course, until one brilliant scholar does, but then the other scholars make fun of him for 'not having enough evidence' and 'nursing a pet theory for thirty years', but once they read it in a book they won't be laughing anymore! They won't be laughing anymore at all!!"

"Yeah probably," says the jester. "Probably they'll stop laughing then." He rubs his finger along the wide edge of his blade, menacingly. "But you still owe me one last rhyming couplet."

You clear your throat nervously, and begin . . .

• I'm packed and I'm stacked, 'specially in the back . . . **Turn to 86**
• Roses can be red, violets are violet, not blue . . . **Turn to 83**
• A certain servant of wise understanding hath said, Let thy heart be of good cheer, O prince . . . **Turn to 85**

75 You frown, absent-mindedly biting your thumb as you ponder your decision. Suddenly you hear a booming voice in your head, just as clearly as if someone were standing directly beside you. "NICE TRY", the voice says, "BUT YOU'RE NOT GETTING OUT OF IT THAT EASILY."

You spit out your own thumb in disgust.

• Okay whatever, go to Denmark: **Turn to 97**
• Check out this Venice place: **Turn to 91**

76 The jester stabs you so much that at the end, you're mostly holes. There's very few people who could survive this, and aging playwrights aren't one of them. After you die one of your friends, James Mabbe, writes that he wonders how come you "went'st so soon / From the world's stage to the grave's tiring room."

It's because you sucked at making poems in the woods, Shakespeare. That's how come.

THE END

77 During the sinking, the crew rushes to the lifeboats. You might expect that there's not enough lifeboats, but quite the opposite: there's AMPLE boats here, Sam. So much so that you have your choice of vessel.

Do you want to get on a boat with the captain and five other members of the bridge crew, or take your chances on a private lifeboat?

• Share a boat with others: **Turn to 93**
• Get my own boat: **Turn to 79**

78 You go inside and chat with Antonio. He hires you on the spot. The next day you ship out on one of his boats, the S.S. *Unsinkable II*.

Three weeks later, the boat sinks.

• Aw man: Turn to 77

79 You board an empty lifeboat and settle in. You and the people aboard the other lifeboats watch the *Unsinkable II* slip beneath the waves forever.

"I really should've wondered why there was a SECOND ship named *Unsinkable*," you mutter to yourself.

Every lifeboat rigs its tiny sail, and together the tiny fleet sets off for the nearest shore. Unfortunately, soon afterwards a gale separates you from the group.

• Try to rejoin the group: Turn to 81

80 Yep. Sorry, Sam. You all draw lots, and yours is the short stick. Nobody is happy about this, but you feel a sense of inevitability.

You try to make it easy for your shipmates. You tell them to think of themselves not as "cannibals" but "canniPALS", since you're all helping each other survive. You tell them that yes, the law is not on their side if they eat your thumb – not to mention rest of your body – but that the public will understand the dire straits you were in when you made this decision. You tell them you face your fate willingly.

What happens next is super gross, I'm sorry to say. Actually, I'm sorry about this whole storyline! This started out with an at least REASONABLY wacky butler taking a vacation, and now it's ending when a lifeboat – empty, save for a single dead body and a large number of bleached, shattered bones – washes up on an uninhabited volcanic island in the Azores!

Geez! Who'd EVER want to read a story that starts out a delightful comedy but then ends up a horrible death-filled tragedy??

THE END

(. . . or is it?) Turn to 173

81 You keep an eye out for the other lifeboats, but you never spot them again. Luckily, the gale has blown your ship into a trade wind, and you find yourself making strong progress every day. It isn't long before you spot land!

As you make your way towards it, your lifeboat is smashed on some offshore rocks, but it's not a big deal. You just swim! No problem!

As you're pulling your drenched body up onto the sandy shore, you look around, trying to determine where you are. You spot a nearby sign, which fills you with relief. That means people live here! You inspect it, and determine it's written in Danish, which – luckily for both you AND this story – you understand fluently!

"DENMARK BEACH" it says. "A GREAT PLACE TO COME OUT OF YOUR 'SHELL.'"

Hey: it's Denmark! You were totally almost gonna visit this place anyway! Nice!! You stroll up to the nearby village, ready to get your vacation started, for REAL this time.

• Go explore Denmark: Turn to 98

82 You tread water some more as you gaze towards the horizon. Nothing but an indifferent ocean meets your gaze.

- Continue treading water: Turn to 96
- Give up: Turn to 112

83 "Roses can be red," you say,
"Violets are violet, not blue
Poem now haiku."

The jester stares at you hard, and then laughs. "Amazing! You took what you already knew was my favourite poetic form and turned it into ANOTHER poetic form, which I gather from context is called 'haiku'!"

"Yes," you say, "for I am the greatest writer that ever lived, so it's no big deal for me to be inspired by traditional Japanese poetry and convert it into English, giving all verses a 5-7-5 syllable structure. Even if this poetic form would normally only arrive to English speakers many centuries from now, I, William Shakespeare, am clearly ahead of the game."

"No doubt about that!" the jester says, clearly delighted to learn new things from a stranger in the woods. "You've definitely earned your life today, Shakespeare!"

- Survive to be Shakespeare another day: Turn to 110

84 Before the jester can say anything, you blurt out "I'm the best writer that ever lived, right?"

"Right," the jester agrees. "You're William Shakespeare."

"So therefore of course it makes sense that I can write poems from the future. THAT IS OBVIOUSLY WHAT THE BEST WRITER WHO EVER LIVED COULD DO. And that," you say, "is what we've already agreed I am."

"Aha," says the jester. "An ontological argument for Shakespeare. I accept it."

"Great," you say, "especially since now that I wrote those rhymes first, that makes ME the author."

"Yes," says the jester. "I accept this. But there's still one problem."

"What's that?" you say.

"YOUR POEM WAS IN AN CCDD RHYMING SCHEME!" he shouts, furious. "OR MAYBE IT WAS AN CCDC SCHEME! I DON'T REMEMBER! BUT IT WASN'T IN THE CDCD FORM IT WAS SUPPOSED TO BE!!"

- Get stabbed by the jester: Turn to 76

85 "A certain servant of wise understanding hath said," you say, "Let thy heart be of good cheer, O prince. Verily we have arrived at our homes. The mallet hath been grasped, and the anchor-post hath been driven into the ground, and the bow of the boat hath grounded on the bank. Thanksgivings have been offered up to God, and every man hath embraced his neighbour."

"Waaaait a second," the jester says. "Wait a second! Is this 'The Tale of the Shipwrecked Traveller'?! SHAKESPEARE, this story is from 2500 B.C.! Entire CIVILIZATIONS have risen and fallen since this story was written! And YES, while it may have been written in a poetic format in its original Hieratic script on ANCIENT EGYPTIAN PAPYRUS, none of those lines rhyme when translated into modern English, which of course is what we call the language we're speaking!"

"Forsooth!" he adds.

He's so upset with your crappy poem that he stabs you right there, on the spot.

- Get stabbed by the jester: Turn to 76

86 The jester's eyes narrow. He makes you turn around so he can see your butt. "Indeed you are . . . " he says, and then after a long moment he adds "Indeed you are." He looks to you, then to his sword, then slowly back to you again.

"Well, I suppose you have met the terms of our bargain," he says. "Congratulations, I'll let you live!"

- Survive to be Shakespeare another day: Turn to 110

87 You tread water some more as you gaze towards the horizon. Nothing but an indifferent ocean meets your gaze.

- Continue treading water: Turn to 82
- Give up: Turn to 112

88 Just as you begin writing you realize: hey, I'm writing a simultaneous prequel AND sequel, why not get more daring? Why not decide that this new book is a sequel NOT to the version of *Hamlet* you wrote, but a BETTER version, a thousand-times more awesome hypothetical version where instead of everyone dying at the end, Ophelia decided everyone sucked and killed them all herself!

"This sounds awesome," you whisper to yourself, "and my one regret is that I don't have time to go back and actually publish this new and fixed version of *Hamlet*, where Ophelia doesn't drown herself in a stupid river over a ridiculous boy, but instead takes control of her destiny, and, having done that, does nothing but kill fools."

You think it over.

"Yes, having Ophelia kill everyone in *Hamlet* is an objective improvement," you say, and begin writing your book with that assumption in place. Within a few weeks, you're done! You call it *How Samuel Ampson Got His Thumb Bit*, because you always loved that bit about biting thumbs in *Romeo and Juliet*. You commission a bunch of illustrations, send it off to the printer, and within a few weeks, copies come back.

They're so good. They're in pristine condition, and not even a little bit cursed! It's actually more about Ophelia than Sam, but whatever, Ophelia rules forever in your both humble and correct opinion.

• Read the book I just wrote: Turn to 89
• Naw, I know what I wrote. I have written my ultimate book, and there are no more mountains left to climb, no more lands left to conquer . . . except one. I, William Shakespeare, have never once in my life punched a shark, and I would like to go do that now please: Turn to 15

89 You open the book you wrote and begin to read:

THAT TIME SAMUEL AMPSON GOT HIS THUMB BIT
a choose-your-own-path adventure

Welcome to *That Time Samuel Ampson Got His Thumb Bit*! Before we begin, there are three things you should know. I, William Shakespeare, have listed them below in increasing order of importance:

THING ONE: This story is a sequel to *Hamlet*, so the first thing you should know is reading this tiny mini-adventure requires you to read a whole other play beforehand. Hah hah hah, sorry!! (Also I changed the ending so Ophelia kills everyone, so uh try to keep that in mind.)

THING TWO: This story is also a PREQUEL to *Romeo and Juliet*, so even after you finish it, there's still a whole other book for you to read. Again: I'm paid by the book here, so all I can do is apologize.

THING THREE: I, William Shakespeare, LOVE living up to the promise of my titles, so our eponymous "Samuel Ampson" is DEFINITELY getting his thumb bit in this story. But the circumstances under which that will happen are entirely up to you! I can promise that there are at least a handful of ways in which you can get your thumb (at least a little) bit non-horribly. Let's see if you can find them!

• Begin the adventure: Turn to 90

90 You are Samuel Ampson! You live in Verona, and you are a heterosexual man who works as a butler for another heterosexual man. I know, this already sounds PRETTY BORING, but let me throw you a curveball: you are about to go on VACATION.

Yes! You are leaving your duties as "guy who moves swords around for my boss, Mr. Capulet" behind – a job which has given you both a +2 perk to buttling (that's what butlers do), as well as a +5 bonus to your "good at smiling even when you don't mean it" stat (you have been working in the service industry for a long time) – and, for the next little while, you are going to see someplace NEW.

You've just put in your last day of work before your trip, eaten a delicious dinner, spent a night lying in a bed involuntarily imagining largely-incoherent fan fiction about the people you know (this is called "dreaming" and everyone keeps telling you it's "normal") and now it's VACATION O'CLOCK.

You've been entertaining two possibilities for your trip. The first is having a "staycation", which is a word you just made up that boils down to "why travel overseas when you can ride two towns over and see Venice?" Venice is a town where they use rivers instead of streets, and giant sticks instead of paddles! That's what you've heard, anyway. It all sounds very exciting.

The alternative is going to Denmark, which you've heard has some delightful little hamlets that are well worth visiting. Plus, Denmark has lots of rad beaches, cheap beer, AND castles! You would love to drink inexpensive beer while touring a castle on a beach. That sounds great!

So where will it be? Where will you go on vacation, Samuel Ampson?

• Go to Venice: **Turn to 91**
• Go to Denmark: **Turn to 97**
• Bite your thumb anxiously as you ponder the decision: **Turn to 75**

91 You hop on "Thunderhoof Starsparkles" – a horse loaned to you by Lord Capulet, which, to answer your question, WAS indeed named by his daughter Juliet when she was six – and begin the ride to Venice. The ride takes the better part of a day, so on the way you pass the time by making up little rhymes. Here's one of them:

"Here I am upon my horse
Soon to Venice in due course
Maybe there I'll find a source
Of some sexy intercourse"

Sam!! That's not an appropriate poem! I had no idea butlers could be so RUDE when alone on the middle of a forest trail!!

You apologize for your steamy erotic poetry and compose a more appropriate poem:

"Here I am upon my steed
Off to Venice my horse leads
Maybe there I'll fill my need
For some sort of sexy deed"

SAMUEL A. AMPSON, dang dude, you need to lower your expectations for this vacation or you're gonna be really disappointed!!

• Arrive in Venice, horny: Turn to 92

92 You arrive in Venice and it's okay, I guess. It's okay! You'd heard about how they have rivers instead of streets but you'd thought that ALL their streets would be like that. Not so. There are plenty of ordinary streets. You feel a little disappointed! It feels a little familiar! You're worried this vacation is turning out to be a dud!

You're wandering Venice, poking your head into places that look touristy, when you wander by a local merchant's establishment. A flier on the door reads:

HATH NOT A WORKER EYES?
If he does, he must surely notice this EXCELLENT OPPORTUNITY

to join ANTONIO'S MERCHANT FLEET!!

— see the world! —
— meet interesting people! —
— sell them stuff for me! —

If you are ABLE-BODIED and POLITE and GOOD AT
SELLING UNSPECIFIED GOODS, join me!

ENQUIRE WITHIN

Why, this sounds like just the sort of thing to spruce up your time off, Sam: a job! After all, this is your first vacation and you don't feel like you're particularly good at it. And this new job would still be LIKE a vacation, since it is technically a vacation from the job you already have!

This could be just the thing you're looking for, Sam!

• Go inside and get a job: Turn to 78
• What? No, I'm here to RELAX. Stay in Venice! Turn to 114

93 You board the captain's lifeboat and settle in. Together, you watch *Unsinkable II* slip beneath the waves forever.

"Do you think they'll build another one?" someone asks.

"Plenty of numbers left in the Roman numeral system," the captain mutters.

Every lifeboat rigs its tiny sail, and together the tiny fleet sets off for the nearest shore. Unfortunately, soon afterwards a gale separates your bridge-crew lifeboat from everyone else.

• Try to rejoin the group: Turn to 94

94 You keep an eye out for the other lifeboats, but you never spot them again. Worse, you soon find yourself becalmed in the middle of the ocean, stuck under a beating sun, with few supplies, little water, and very little hope. With no wind to fill your sails, all you can do is wait. You and the rest of the crew weaken with each passing day.

And your hunger is growing.

Pretty soon, someone suggests that maybe cannibalism isn't so bad after all. You're all so hungry that you agree. One could be sacrificed to save the rest. You decide to draw lots.

• Aw man! I'm gonna get my thumb bit, aren't I?? Turn to 80

95 You enter into Verona, passing the Verona Geyser on your way south towards the downtown. Unfortunately, you run head-first into a mob of Veronans, who attack you on sight. You attack them too, but here is the thing: while you're a murder scientist on horseback, they're LITERALLY an angry mob. Their whole thing is overpowering people through sheer numbers!

Sadly, that's what they do to you and Sam. The last thing you see is one of them biting his thumb (it's weird) before someone manages to knock you over and stab you right in the organs!

There's actually several organs you can live without: technically you only need ONE kidney, for example, and the spleen helps fight infections but you can survive without it, your appendix is such a small deal we're not even sure why it's there, and reproductive organs are basically optional, ESPECIALLY if you don't want to have kids.

Those aren't the organs they stab you in.

To see what that looks like, turn the page

(. . . or is it?) Turn to 173

96 You tread water some more as you gaze towards the horizon. Nothing but an indifferent ocean meets your gaze.

• Continue treading water: Turn to 87
• Give up: Turn to 112

97 You don't waste any time, and hop on the first boat you find that just happens to be headed down the River Adige, through Verona, out into the Adriatic Sea, around the boot of Italy, past the Strait of Gibraltar, around Spain, past France, and through the North Sea past Denmark. Your haste at boat-choosing begins to feel like a mistake when you find out you're on the S.S. *Aqua-Holic Nauti Buoy*, but it ends up feeling like a good decision later on when you barely avoid a storm that seems destined to become a devastating gale. Had you delayed your travels, you would've ended up right in the middle of it! Looks like the fates are smiling on (this particular version of) you, Sam!

When you arrive at Denmark, it turns out you didn't pay for the kind of ticket that lets the boat stop for you to get off, but rather the cheaper sort of ticket that has them toss you overboard when you get close. You do make it to shore, drenched, tired, and, to be fair, more in need of a vacation than ever!

You stroll up to the nearby village, ready to get your vacation started.

• Explore Denmark: **Turn to 98**

98 The village is – well, it's empty. There's buildings, roads, city squares – but nobody's IN them. You'd say that it looks like everyone here just decided to up and move somewhere else, except you keep coming across bloodstains all over the dang place.

Saying it's "unsettling" is putting it mildly, and as an author, my job is to make things as NON-mild as possible, so let me try this again:

All human life has been expunged from the village, and it looks like they didn't go willingly. Unnatural bloodstains coat walls, furniture, ceilings. An eerie silence hangs over everything. The open doors of buildings creak in the wind, exposing their dead insides slowly being reclaimed by an indifferent nature. You're about to explore one when you hear a twig snap behind you. Someone – or something – is creeping there. You freeze, feeling the hairs on the back of your neck stand up, and whatever is behind you freezes too.

There! That's MUCH better.

Anyway, you turn around and can't find anyone, and the village is hecka weird, and you can't find any bodies, and it looks like Denmark isn't going to be the vacation you'd hoped.

There's a castle at the top of the hill in the middle of town. It seems that if you're going to find any answers, you'll find them there!

• Explore castle: **Turn to 99**

99 You poke your head in the castle, and you're like, "Oh, THAT'S where all the bodies are! Duh!" This place is filled with bodies, Sam.

It's actually extremely gross, but people died here, so when you drop an involuntary vom at how gross everything is, you try to make it the most respectful vom you can.

You succeed about as well as can be expected.

You shout to see if anyone is there, but don't receive a response. Using your keen buttling senses (that perk came in handy after all!), you quickly discern from the layout of the rooms where the logical location of the throne room would be. You make your way towards it, and there, in that throne room that's also surrounded by dead bodies, you see something you're not expecting: a young woman, dressed in blue, sitting on the throne.

"Hey," she says.

• Talk to woman: **Turn to 100**
• Run away screaming: **Turn to 113**

100 "Greetings," you say. "I'm Samuel Ampson, butler." You summon all of your +5 to smiling stat in order to smile in a way that you hope is non-enraging.

It seems to work!

"Ophelia," she says. "This is my home. What are you doing here?"

"Um . . . ," you say, "I'm on . . . vacation?"

"Vacation," she repeats. "You're vacationing here. In Denmark. In my castle. Which is full of the bodies of everyone who has ever wronged me."

"I didn't know about that stuff when I decided to come here," you say.

"Yes, well," Ophelia says, standing up, "I'm sure you thought 'Oh, Denmark! Who KNOWS what's gone on in that place since I was last there! Why, any NUMBER of possible timelines could've taken place, leaving the current state of Denmark in quantum flux, only becoming fixed when I observe it!'"

"Beg pardon?" you say. "Huh? I've never been here before."

"Maybe it'll be the place where everyone lived happily ever after after all and I got to invent internal heating!" she says, ranting. "Maybe it's the one where I beat up Gertrude and got a big muscley arm!"

"I don't–" you begin, then stop. "Who is Gertrude?"

"Who WAS Gertrude," Ophelia says. "Because she's dead now. She died due to overdosing on being killed by me. Just like Horatio, just like Reynaldo, just like Polonius, just like Fortinbras. All dead."

You have no idea who these people are. You just got here!

Ophelia picks up a sword and spins it in her hand, casually, testing its weight. "I've been researching here, Sam," she says. "Finally I have time to FOCUS. No distractions."

She points the sword at you.

"Except for you," she says.

"Um," you say. As you tuck your thumbs safely into your pockets, you have the distinct feeling that you're in trouble.

• Apologize for intruding: Turn to 101
• Aw geez I'm so dead, I might as well go out making the most offensive gesture I can: Turn to 116

101 You apologize and explain you didn't mean to bother her. Ophelia looks like she's about to kill you with that sword she's carrying, but thinking quickly, you point over her shoulder and shout "Oh my god, what's THAT?!"

Ophelia looks behind her. "That's my throne," she says. "Of skulls, mostly, but also a lot of ribs. I'm the Queen here."

"Delightful!" you say, hoping to keep her talking. "What do you do for fun?"

"Oh, this and that," Ophelia says. "Like I said: I research. Science stuff, you know? I'm real good at it."

"But what about your time off?" you ask.

"Puzzles, I guess," Ophelia says. "I make crosswords and then try to forget the clues and solve them. Or I make mazes. I built a corn maze out back."

"Neat!" you say.

"Only there wasn't any corn, so it's constructed out of giant stacks of dead bodies," she says.

"Oh," you say. You think this sounds – kind of horrible, actually, living alone surrounded by gross corpses. You begin to feel empathy! You start to think that if YOU were in her position, maybe you'd like a vacation from all this, a vacation someplace different, like, say – Verona??

You're about to invite her to come back to Verona with you for a little vacation of her own, when you remember SHE'S the one responsible for all this killing in the first place! Wait, so maybe it's not the best idea to invite her along?

Heck man, I don't know! Lucky thing it's not up to me, huh??

• Invite Ophelia to come back to Verona with you: Turn to 102
• No that's crazy, just get out of here: Turn to 115

102 You try to convince Ophelia to come back to Verona with you, but she's not into it. She says she doesn't need a vacation. She says she likes it here.

• Tell her about Verona's lovely vistas: Turn to 103

103 She's not convinced.

• Tell her about Verona's terrific culture and/or nightlife: Turn to 106

104 Right, you are now Ophelia! You are an extremely competent young woman, gifted in the sciences, and after some unfortunate events that don't need detailing here (but could be explored more fully in a book called *To Be or Not To Be*, if indeed such a thing existed, listen: no promises, but maybe check your local book retailer just to be sure) you've turned your considerable talents towards murder, and now nobody here is alive anymore except you!

Hey, random thought: maybe a vacation would be just the thing you need!

• I am suddenly convinced that a vacation is just the thing I need: Turn to 105

105 Great! Terrific! And lucky for you, you've got a visitor, Sam, who wants you to come back with him to Verona for just such a vacation.

You tell him you're suddenly big into vacations, and he's happy to hear it. He leads you down to the beach, where he tells you that you'll hail a passing boat and take it to Verona. "It'll be fine," he says. "Boats rarely sink these days."

"I've got a really good feeling about this," he adds.

You stare out across the ocean. "You know that Verona is accessible by land from Denmark, right?" you ask. "It's basically due south of here." Sam looks at you. He did not know that.

"I knew that," he says.

You go to your stables, select your two finest steeds, and you and Sam ride to Verona.

• Ride to Verona: Turn to 107

106 No dice.

• Really? Did she not hear me about the vistas? Tell her about the vistas again: **Turn to 103**
• Look, we could be at this all day, just BE Ophelia and decide to come back with me to Verona! **Turn to 104**

107
Upon arriving, you discover some bad news: Verona has invested in some new border security measures. Well, "invested" is probably too strong a word, since these security measures are basically just three mobs of Veronans patrolling the city, looking for people without the right papers.

Unfortunately, you didn't bring any papers with you (plus you killed the Danish border authority a while back, so: two problems), and Sam explains that his must've gotten lost while he was swimming. So, no matter what happens, you're in this together.

You and your mighty steed pause at the entrance to the city. What'll it be, Ophelia?

• Man, whatever, I'll just kill anyone who gets in my way! PROCEED: **Turn to 95**
• Investigate further: **Turn to 108**

108
Before entering Verona, you tie up your horse and climb a tree to get a better look at the security measures you'll be dealing with.

You see three routes into the city, each close enough that you'll be able to ride between them easily. Route one – to the west – is the residential path, going through a playground, past Verona Dam, and by some nice houses. Route two – in the middle – is the scenic route, taking you past a geyser, a small hill, and across the sunny beaches of the River Adige. Finally, route three – to the east – is the commercial path, taking you past Verona Farmer's Market, City Hall, and some public tennis courts.

After scouting out the terrain, you locate the mobs and observe their movements. Luckily, they're moving predictably. Climbing down, you produce the follow diagram for Sam:

<pre>
            US
            |
          x x M
          x M x
          M x x
            |
        HOME FREE
</pre>

"US is where we are, and HOME FREE is where we want to be," you say. "If we can make it there, we'll be in the downtown core, out of the area the mobs are searching. You'll be able to get us some new papers from your boss, right?"

Sam nods.

"So here's what we're dealing with," you say, referring again to the diagram. "The Xs represent locations we can travel to, and each M represents a location with a mob in it right now. The mobs are travelling in straight lines, north and south, up and down, entering a new location at regular intervals. But they're moving quietly, so as to surprise anyone they come across. They all moving north, but the mob at the right, having gone as far north as they can, has now reversed and is moving south. The others will do the same shortly, back and forth, back and forth"

"Ah," Sam says.

"So," you say, getting back onto your horse, "since we know where we're entering, and we know where we want to end up, and we know the direction and method in which the mobs are moving, it's easy enough to come up with a series of moves that will allow us to navigate this labyrinth without encountering any mobs."

"Ah," Sam says. He stares at the map, then at you, then at the map again. Then he furrows his brow. He looks like he wants to bite his thumb.

You sigh. "Look, just follow me," you say.

• Enter Verona: Turn to 109

108

109 As you walk into town, the gates behind you close with a click. They're locked, Ophelia. You and Sam won't be able to get out the way you got in.

Alright, science and logic lady: let's find how smart you really are! Verona Geyser is just ahead.

• Continue towards the geyser: Turn to 126

110 The jester turns to leave.

"I can't wait to tell everyone that THE William Shakespeare wrote a poem both ABOUT me and FOR me, and all I had to do was hold him at knifepoint here in these yellow woods!"

"Yes, well, you're welcome," you say.

You return home, relieved, and here's the thing: you never write another word again, Shakespeare. That poem you wrote in the woods was so great, so spectacular, that you know you'll never be able to top it. It's so good, in fact, that you don't even try to punch sharks anymore either! Instead you rest, secure in the knowledge that as long as this one poem survives then your entire career will have been worth it. It won't – on his way home the jester falls and gets stuck and dies and eventually turns into a scary skeleton – but there's no way you could possibly know that!

THE END

P.S. Also, if we're being completely honest with ourselves, it wasn't even that good a poem. It was all over the place, Shakespeare. Come on, man. Pull up your socks.

111 As you make your way forward, you literally bump into the very obstacle you've been trying to avoid: an angry mob! Here's the bad news: they pile up on top of you and Sam in a giant heap, which crushes you both into a chunky paste. You're about to say "Wait a minute, I don't understand how you could practically do that, given that t–" but that's as far as you get before you're, as I say, reduced to a chunky paste.

• Oh well. Turn to 169

112 You consider what choices you've made that led you to this moment: your impulsiveness, your eagerness, your obsessive desire to punch a shark, but it's no good: try as you might, you can't find any fault in any of them. All of your choices were objectively correct and blameless!

But your muscles are screaming. Your whole body is tired, exhausted in a way you've never felt before. You, finally, at long last, have nothing left to give.

You relax. You sigh.

And you sink beneath the waves.

THE END

113 You run away screaming, but the woman quickly catches up to you, and as she's stabbing you to death, explains how her name is Ophelia and her game is killing anyone who bothers her. It's this whole thing, she says. Long story, she says.

All the stabs are quickly turning you into an ex-Sam, but you're confused. Didn't I say you'd get your thumb bit? You can't die until that happens, right? And honestly, I understand where you're coming from. The catch is, I never said you'd be ALIVE when your thumb got bit, and once you die a lot of bacteria and other scavengers are going to feed on your body, including your thumb. Sorry dude. Circle of life.

Your boss is mildly inconvenienced when you never return from vacation, but fills the position in short order.

THE END

(. . . or is it?) Turn to 173

P.S. You become a ghost and end up meeting a bunch of other cool Denmark ghosts! There's ghosts of KINGS here, Sam. And their brothers! And they squabble with each other! It turns out that relationship drama is super interesting when you're not involved in it, and you get to spend several thousand years hearing some very juicy gossip. Yay! You agree you are extremely satisfied with this ending.

114 You've already got ONE job that you're here trying to find even the briefest respite from, and that's plenty, thank you! So instead you stick around in Venice. It's nice enough: you spend a lot of pleasant afternoons in café patios, reading and enjoying fine Italian coffee.

During one of these pleasant afternoons, a mosquito bites you! RIGHT ON YOUR THUMB.

You gasp. The prophecy came true! In a super boring way!! This is great! You spend the rest of your vacation relieved and at one point even manage to have that sexual intercourse you were writing poems about earlier! It's kind of impressive you pulled this off, considering how you're the type of guy who writes poems to himself about how much he wants to have sex, but there was someone in Venice who was big into it.

When your vacation ends, you hop back on Thunderhoof Starsparkles and ride back to Verona, extremely satisfied. You feel recharged! You can't wait to get back into buttling!

On your first day back on the job, you're carrying swords for your master when you run into two of the hated Montagues. As they walk by you wave happily, too relaxed to get into a fight right now.

They wave back, suspicious, but nothing more comes of the matter, and that's the last you hear from those two particular gentlemen of Verona. You live happily ever after and your thumb never gets bit again, except a couple times during a sex thing that you both gave enthusiastic and ongoing consent to.

THE END

(. . . or is it?) **Turn to 173**

P.S. Yes, that last second-to-last sentence IS a shout out another book in this series, *The Two Gentleman of Verona . . . Or Are They? Gentlemen, I Mean? You Decide (Because This Is One Of Those Books Where You Decide What Happens)*

P.P.S. We will absolutely not be shortening the title.

115 You make your excuses, promise not to bother Ophelia again, and leave feeling that you are missing out on a lot of backstory here, including who Ophelia is, what her deal is, how she got so good at killing everyone, and what possible motivation she'd have for doing so!

"If only," you say, going back to the beach, "if only the backstory I craved was available in some convenient format, perhaps even in a book, that I might read it while relaxing on this very beach."

Sadly, this is not a thing that is possible, and we should all stop thinking about it.

You hang out on the beach for a pleasant afternoon – but pretty soon you've had enough of Denmark. When a boat sails by in the late afternoon (the S.S. *Berth Of A Nation*), you:

• Swim out to it and explain your circumstances: Turn to 164
• Go back to Ophelia, I really wish she'd come back to Verona with me: Turn to 102

116 Aha! You're a smart one, Sam. You've realized that in this time period (which, as you know, is the present) there exists an EXTREMELY offensive gesture you can make, and you've got all you need to make it, right here on your human body!

"Who's got two thumbs and isn't afraid of you?" you say. "This guy." Then you put both thumbs in your mouth, and – without breaking eye contact with Ophelia – bite them. You bite them both right at her. This is very rude for anyone to do, much less a butler – but in doing so, you've fulfilled the prophecy of this book! Your thumbs just got bit! Let's see how it's working out for you, huh?

Aw no. Aw geez. In the time it took me to explain all that thumb biting stuff she's already killed you and tossed your body on the pile.

Sorry Sam. If it's any consolation, I'd say this ending gets . . . a THUMBS down?

THE END

To see what that looks like, turn the page

(. . . or is it?) **Turn to 173**

P.S. I'm also sorry about that "thumbs down" joke; I know you just died and I should be more respectful, sorry again

117 That night, your boat sinks.

• Aw geez: **Turn to 119**

118 You get on the S.S. *Berth of a Nation*, again, explain the situation to the captain, again, look forward to Verona, again, and that night your boat sinks. AGAIN. What a shocker, huh?

As you slip beneath the waves on your way to a grim future where fish will nibble on your body (including your thumb: called it!), you feel certain that I'll give you a second do-over. Sorry, Sam. You and I are past your do-over days.

You die relatively horribly, and I feel bad for you, but I'm really not sure what you thought would happen.

THE END

(. . . or is it?) Turn to 173

P.S. Later on, your skull gets hooked on a fishing line and really spooks a fisherman when he reels it in; it's a pretty good prank and I'm sorry you weren't there to see it.

119 There's no lifeboats in it either! Eventually you drown, and when that happens fish nibble on you (including your thumb: CALLED IT).

You die, but I feel bad for you, so I'll let you take back a move. How could you have known that boat was going to sink? That's hardly fair, right? Right!

Okay, so you're back hanging out on the beach during that pleasant afternoon we were talking about – but pretty soon, again, you've had enough of Denmark! When a boat sails by in the late afternoon (the S.S. *Berth Of A Nation*), you:

• Swim out to it and explain your circumstances: Turn to 118
• Wait for the next boat, this boat is baloney: Turn to 120
• Say "FINE, I'LL TAKE OPHELIA WITH ME", go back to her, and suggest she take a vacation in Verona: Turn to 102

120 Your new boat sinks too.

• Aw for crying out loud: **Turn to 124**

121 This new boat sinks almost immediately!

• FRIG: **Turn to 125**

122 The playground is, surprisingly, not the greatest spot for a woman and a butler with their horses to hide out.

You're swarmed by kids who run up, asking if they can pet your horses, asking if they can ride your horses, asking if YOU can get down on all fours so they can ride you, and so on. You make the mistake of doing it for one of them, and now they all want rides. They're screaming for rides.

"Shh," you say on all fours as several kids pile on to your back, "kids, be quiet. I'M ON A STEALTH MISSION."

Their screaming quiets a little, I guess?

• Hide out here for a bit, this playground rules: **Turn to 128**
• Go south: Verona Dam is the perfect place to hide! **Turn to 140**
• Go east: hide behind the famous Geyser of Verona that Erupts on the Regular: **Turn to 129**

123 The confusion and spectacle of your boat sinking in Verona Harbour just as you're disembarking from it works to your advantage in a couple of ways. It distracts the border guards, which is great because you lost your papers a while back (it happened while you were swimming to Denmark the first time, sorry for not mentioning this sooner), and it ALSO distracts the three angry mobs patrolling the city looking for people trying to sneak into Verona without papers (sorry again, I was going to give you a heads up about them soon, honest).

You return to Capulet Castle, and announce your return to your employer, Lord Capulet. He is happy to see you, and you are happy to see him. You do your best work as a butler, and it's nice to be your best self again. Also it's nice to be on boats that don't sink all the time.

Several weeks later, you and another butler are moving a giant pile of Lord Capulet's swords from his Sword Storeroom to his Secondary Sword Storeroom when you come across some competing butlers, working for the hated Montagues. You get into an argument and end up biting your thumb directly at them. This gesture is extremely rude, and as such they want to kill you, but thankfully this dude named Benvolio intervenes to try to keep the peace.

And that, Samuel Ampson, is how in the end you got your thumb bit after all! Just a wee li'l bite that you did yourself to make a stranger angry. It's the best we could've hoped for!

As you leave after the fight, you notice a young man in the distance. He looks a little sad, I guess. And you don't know it, but his name is "Romeo" and I've written a whole other book about him! YES! If this entirely disposable character now given a throwaway mention at the end of this story has you, the reader, salivating for more, then boy howdy, have I got good news for you!

The book is called *Romeo and Juliet* and it's available wherever books are sold, unless it's later in which case it's available wherever USED books that people bought before they decided they didn't want them anymore are sold, unless it's later in which case it's in that big pile of rubble and books which is all that remains of your local library after the coming of Zorglax 85300, unless it's later in which case it's available in the archives of Zorglax 85301, where you will find it filed under "The Only Thing We Kept From Planet Earth, And We Don't Even Know Why".

Good luck!!

123

THE END

(. . . or is it?) Turn to 173

124 Okay. This is your last do-over, Sam. Let's take it back a bit.

Once more you find yourself hanging out on the beach in the middle of a very pleasant afternoon, right after you chatted with Ophelia! But again, soon you've had enough of Denmark. When a boat sails by in the late afternoon (the S.S. *Berth Of A Nation*), you:

• Swim out to it and explain your circumstances: Turn to 118
• Skip it, AND skip the next boat, but grab the boat you see after that: Turn to 121
• Say "FINE, I'LL TAKE OPHELIA WITH ME", go back to her, and suggest she take a vacation in Verona: Turn to 102

125 . . . almost immediately after it drops you off safe and sound in Verona, that is!!

• Aw yeah, FINALLY: Turn to 123

126 You conceal Sam, yourself and your horses behind Verona Geyser. It's gurgling right now. Maybe if you stick around it'll explode! Maybe that's a good thing! Maybe not!

• Hide out here for a bit: **Turn to 129**
• Go south: we'll hide behind the hill! **Turn to 162**
• Go east: we'll blend in nicely with all the other horses and humans around Verona Market! **Turn to 130**
• Go west: nobody would look for a couple of adults and horses in a playground! **Turn to 128**

127 The mob bursts into the marketplace, spots you instantly, and pulls you both off your horses by your collars.

Someone puts a dark bag over your head. But just before they do, you see two nearby vendors, oblivious to this drama, smiling, laughing, one telling a joke to the other.

And you've been pulled just far enough away that you can't hear it a word of it. IT'S SO FRUSTRATING, OPHELIA.

• Get carried away by the mob: **Turn to 163**

128 The playground kids start pulling on the hair of your horse. "Hey, how would you like it if I pulled YOUR hair??" you say, and the kids start screaming. Parents and nurses are looking over, concerned. Ophelia, you're about to blow your cover!

"I'm joking, I'm joking! I won't pull your hair!" they say.

The kids stop screaming, but a large subset of them begin crying instead. Near as you can figure they WANTED their hair pulled, they were screaming in joy earlier, and you saying you would and then telling them you won't has upset them greatly.

You're reluctantly pulling on their hair to quiet them down when you think, hey, maybe this isn't the best time to be a strange couple to be in a playground when they don't even have any kids, huh?

- Hide out here for a bit: **Turn to 131**
- Go south: Verona Dam is the perfect place to hide! **Turn to 148**
- Go east: hide behind the famous Geyser of Verona that Erupts on the Regular: **Turn to 132**

129 Your spot behind the geyser isn't the most effective hiding place in the world, especially since you're on horseback and the geyser isn't going off right now.

The mob rushes in from the south, detects you instantly, and before long you and Sam are surrounded. But you're not done yet, Ophelia. Oh no. You've got one last move up your sleeve.

Unfortunately, that last move is labelled "get overwhelmed by an angry mob".

- See where they carry you: **Turn to 163**

130 You trot into Verona Market, confident that you, Sam, and your horses will blend in perfectly amongst the other vendors, customers, and their horses.

There are two vendors here: one's laughing, slapping the other on the back. "Get it?" she's saying. But her friend being slapped isn't reacting: whatever joke she just heard, it was evidently NOT as hilarious as the teller thought it was.

"Okay, no, you're telling it wrong," she says. "Listen, it's way better if you deliver it correctly." A pause, then she smiles.

"Knock knock," she says.

- Stay here, I want to hear where this joke is going: **Turn to 133**
- Go south: hide among the offices of City Hall: **Turn to 145**
- Go west: hide behind the famous Geyser of Verona that Erupts on the Regular: **Turn to 132**

131 The mob of angry Veronans approaches the playground and spots you.

"There they are!" someone shouts. "Let's murder them!" shouts another. "Why are they hiding in a playground with horses?" shouts a third, but before you can answer him (you were going to say "Because I wanted to, DUHHH") the mob descends on you, picking you up and carrying you off into the distance.

• Get carried off by the mob somewhere: Turn to 163

132 Seconds after you hide yourself behind the geyser, it erupts into a spectacular display of nature's raw power that makes your hiding place behind it even better. Wait, sorry, that was a typo. I meant to say that it made your hiding place even WETTER.

We'll correct it in the next edition.

Anyway, you and Sam are drenched now. Your hiding place sucks and is really moist.

• Hide out here for a bit longer: the geyser will die down shortly: Turn to 135
• Go south: we'll hide behind the hill! Turn to 147
• Go east: we'll blend in nicely with all the other horses and humans around Verona Market! Turn to 136
• Go west: nobody would look for some adults and their horses in a playground! Turn to 134

133 You've blended in with the crowd perfectly. There are two vendors here, mid-conversation.

"A knock knock joke?" one says, smiling. "WHAT A SURPRISE. Alright. Who's there?"

• Hide out here for a bit: I want to hear how this joke ends: **Turn to 136**
• Go south: hide among the offices of City Hall: **Turn to 149**
• Go west: hide behind the famous Geyser of Verona that Erupts on the Regular: **Turn to 135**

134 You arrive at the park and look it over. It looks to be a pretty standard park: there's a bunch of kids playing, some parents off to the side chatting with each other while keeping one eye on their kids, and you: a couple of strangers arriving on horseback.

You're a sensation! The kids all run over to you and gape at your horses. You smile and wave to their parents and nurses, collected across the park.

"I'm just a regular lady!" you shout to them. "I definitely haven't committed any murders this week!"

You hold up part of your tunic.

"These are ketchup stains!" you add.

• Hide out here for a bit: **Turn to 122**
• Go south: Verona Dam is the perfect place to hide! **Turn to 137**
• Go east: hide behind the famous Geyser of Verona that Erupts on the Regular: **Turn to 126**

135 The geyser is quiet. You're quiet too, as you and Sam hide behind this tiny wet hole in the ground. Nobody seems to be paying any particular attention to these boring strangers on horseback next to a hole, which is great!

• Hide out here for a bit longer: it's nice here: **Turn to 126**
• Go south: we'll hide behind the hill! **Turn to 138**
• Go east: we'll blend in nicely with all the other horses and humans around Verona Market! **Turn to 127**
• Go west: nobody would look for some adults and their horses in a playground! **Turn to 122**

136 Nobody pays any particular attention to you among the hustle and bustle of the market. There are two vendors nearby, mid conversation. You think you can hear what sounds like boots on a gravel road coming from the south, but on the other hand, it's probably nothing.

"Wendel," says one.
"Wendel who?" says the other.

• Hide out here for a bit: this knock-knock joke is gonna pay off RIGHT NOW: Turn to 127
• Go south: hide among the offices of City Hall: Turn to 171
•Go west: hide behind the famous Geyser of Verona that Erupts on the Regular: Turn to 126

137 You arrive at Verona Dam and blend in easily: there's a crowd of people picnicking at the base, and they brought their horses too, so nobody pays any particular attention to your little posse.

You trot around on your horse in the sunshine, and it's really pleasant. But then you notice someone who has been standing at the base of the dam the entire time you've been here. They're facing the dam, unmoving. It looks like they're touching it. It's eerie.

You're about to approach when you hear what sounds like an angry mob approaching from the south.

• Talk to the person at the base of the dam: Turn to 140
• Go north: nobody would look for some adults and their horses in a playground! Turn to 128
• Go south: there's some housing there and we could probably hide in some random stranger's home, perhaps in a giant wardrobe large enough to two humans and their horses: Turn to 162
• Go east: we'll hide behind the hill! Turn to 141

138 Your attention is focused elsewhere when suddenly you become aware that in the past few seconds you've been surrounded by an extremely angry, extremely violent mob! You're trapped, Ophelia!

You try to reason with them, but they just stick you and Sam in a giant burlap sack.

• Oh well: Turn to 163

139 You and Sam ride your horses into city hall, acting like you have all the reason in the world to do this, trotting down the hallway find an empty office. You lead your horses inside, dismount, and close the door behind you.

A few minutes pass, and you're becoming increasingly aware of a din outside your door. It sounds . . . like smooching? You open the door a crack and peek outside, and all you see are rows and rows of people kissing each other! The entire office building is engaged in one giant smoochfest. You kinda want to join in and see where this goes AND figure out how this even got started in the first place!

• Stay here for a bit: I wanna kiss on some pretty people too: Turn to 142
• Go north: hide out in Verona Market: Turn to 162
• Go south: we'll remain inconspicuous on the tennis courts by playing tennis with our horses: Turn to 155
• Go west: we'll hide behind a hill: Turn to 141

140 Suddenly a mob of angry Veronans arrives from the south, and storming past the dam, spots you. Dozens of hands grab you, pulling you and Sam off your horses and carrying you away somewhere. And I'm sorry Ophelia, but you've got absolutely no choice in the matter!

• Get carried off by the mob somewhere: Turn to 163

141 You tuck yourself and your horses behind the hill and wait. So far, so good! Nobody seems to be paying any attention to the weird strangers and their horses trying to hide behind a small hill in Verona, which I guess says a lot about the kind of town Verona is.
You overhear a man pacing, talking to himself.

"Come on, dummy!" he says. "You can't keep falling in love with every person you meet. And even if you do, you can't come on so strong!!"

He stops in his tracks and looks off away from you.

"Oh my god, there's someone coming. Oh my god, she's GORGEOUS. Even more gorgeous than the last one. You're doing it again, Gary!!"

He sighs in frustration, then looks at her some more, then sighs happily.

"On the other hand," he says, still staring at this woman who hasn't even noticed him yet, "I've got to be me, and I'll never change who I am just to fit in with 'society'!!"

He begins to move toward her.

• Hide out here for a bit: I want to see how this goes for ol' Gary! Turn to 144
• Go north: hide behind the famous Geyser of Verona that Erupts on the Regular: Turn to 148
• Go south: the beach of the Adige River is just the place to lay low for a while: Turn to 157
• Go east: hide among the offices of City Hall: Turn to 145
• Go west: we'll hide by Verona Dam, a large structure that'll distract passers-by from noticing some random boring people on horses: Turn to 143

142 You think sitting in an empty office on horseback is the perfect hiding space, and I guess it kinda was: that is, until the mob showed up and did a quick sweep and caught you in a room from which there is only one exit and there is an angry mob in the way of that exit now.

They pull you and Sam off your horses, put a dark bag on your head, and drag you out of the office. You don't even get to see what the other office dwellers were doing! And it was probably way more interesting than sitting in an empty office on a horse, too!

• Get carried away by the mob: Turn to 163

143 You arrive at Verona Dam and blend in easily: there's a crowd of people picnicking at the base, and they brought their horses too, so nobody pays any particular attention to your little posse.

You trot around on your horse in the sunshine, and it's really pleasant. But then you notice someone who has been standing at the base of the dam the entire time you've been here. They've been facing the dam, unmoving. Then, all of a sudden, they move to leave. And a small spring of water spurts out of the dam behind them.

You're about to intervene when you notice someone else coming up to the person. They meet at a pole set up near the base of the dam, and write their names and the current time on the sheet posted there.

"Five minute break," the person leaving says.

"You know it," the person arriving says. Then she moves towards the hole in the dam and, sticking her finger in, stops the leak.

• Hide out here for a bit: I want to see where this is going: Turn to 146
• Go north: nobody would look for some adults and their horses in a playground! Turn to 111
• Go south: there's some housing there and we could probably hide in some random stranger's home, perhaps in a giant wardrobe large enough to fit two humans and their horses: Turn to 159
• Go east: we'll hide behind the hill! Turn to 147

144 Your attention is focused elsewhere when suddenly you become aware that in the past few seconds you've been surrounded by an extremely angry, extremely violent mob! You're trapped, Ophelia!

You try to reason with them, but they just stick you and Sam in a giant burlap sack.

• Oh dang: Turn to 163

145 You and Sam ride your horses into city hall, acting like you have all the reason in the world to do this, and trotting down the hallway find an empty office. You lead your horses inside, dismount, and close the door behind you.

A few minutes pass, and the office is supremely quiet. That's weird. You open the door a crack and peek outside, but all you see are rows and rows of people, quietly working. Nobody even looks up.

This place is much more boring than you'd hoped!

• Hide out here for a bit: maybe it'll get more interesting: Turn to 149
• Go north: blend in among the shoppers at Verona Market: Turn to 136
• Go south: we'll remain inconspicuous on the tennis courts by playing tennis with our horses: Turn to 111
• Go west: we'll hide behind the hill! Turn to 147

146 Suddenly a mob of angry Veronans arrives from the south, and storming past the dam, spots you. Dozens of hands grab you, pulling you and Sam off your horses and carrying you away somewhere. And I'm sorry Ophelia, but you've got absolutely no choice in the matter!

• Get carried off by the mob somewhere: Turn to 163

147 You tuck yourself and your horses behind the hill and wait. So far, so good! It's not THAT big a hill, but you're at least partially obscured from anyone who is trying to view you and happens to approach from the correct angle.

You see a man running up to a woman, and manage to just barely overhear what they're saying.

"Excuse me, my name's Gary and I know we've just met, but you have to be the most gorgeous person I've ever seen," the man says.

"Excuse me?" she replies.

"I know this is crazy, but – would you like to get dinner with me tonight?"

"What? No. NO THANK YOU," the woman says.

"I feel the same way," Gary replies. "Why play games, you know? I know you can feel this attraction too. Let's throw caution to the wind and get married!"

"EXCUSE ME??" she replies.

"You're right," Gary says, "I'm doing this all wrong, I'm sorry. Let me do this properly," he says, and then gets down on one knee. "Will you marry me?" he says.

• Hide out here for a bit: I want to hear what she says: **Turn to 138**
• Go north: hide behind the famous Geyser of Verona that Erupts on the Regular: **Turn to 126**
• Go south: the beach of the Adige River is just the place to lay low for a while: **Turn to 171**
• Go east: hide among the offices of City Hall: **Turn to 139**
• Go west: we'll hide by Verona Dam, a large structure that'll distract passers-by from noticing some random boring people on horses: **Turn to 137**

148 As you make your way forward, you literally bump into the very obstacle you've been trying to avoid: an angry mob! Here's the bad news: they reduce you and Sam to a chunky mist, to nothing that would not fit through a sieve. You're about to say "Wait a minute, I don't understand how you could practically do that, given that y–" but that's as far as you get before you're, as I say, reduced to nothing that would not fit through a sieve.

• Oh well. **Turn to 169**

149 You think sitting in an empty office on horseback is the perfect hiding space, and I guess it kinda was. That is, until the mob showed up and did a quick sweep and caught you in a room from which there is only one exit and there is an angry mob in the way of that exit now.

They pull you and Sam off your horses, put a dark bag on your head, and drag you out of the office. You don't even get to see what the other office dwellers were doing! And it was probably way more interesting than sitting in an empty office on a horse, too!

• Get carried away by the mob: **Turn to 163**

150 You peek out through a crack in the door to see what's going on outside the safety of your giant, surprisingly spacious wardrobe.

You notice a man sleeping on his couch, happily, when suddenly a mob of angry Verona citizens bursts through the door and tears through the house. I think they're looking for you, Ophelia!

One man pulls open the wardrobe and finds you inside it. "I found them!" he shouts! The next thing you know is the sensation of dozens of hands grabbing at you and Sam, pulling you off your horses and out into the street.

Throughout it all, the guy on the couch doesn't even stir. MAN. That guy has it figured out, I gotta say!!

• Confront the angry mob: **Turn to 163**

151 You and Sam blend in with all the couples going for romantic horseback rides on the beach by just discreetly trotting alongside another couple and allowing everyone else who sees you to assume the four of you are on a double date, or perhaps even in a polyamorous relationship, or are at the very least friends with benefits wherein everyone keeps clear and open lines of communication with everyone else involved!

You notice a little girl beginning to work on a sandcastle. Judging by the debris around her, it's rising from the remains of a previous, smaller castle that was destroyed very recently. This one looks like it'll be about 10% larger than whatever came before.

Not bad, little girl! Not bad at all!

• Go south, escape the mobs!! **Turn to 167**

• Hide out here for a bit: I want to see this castle get built: **Turn to 154**
• Go north: there's a hill there we could hide behind: **Turn to 141**
• Go east: we'll remain inconspicuous on the tennis courts by playing tennis with our horses: **Turn to 155**
• Go west: there's some housing there and we could probably hide in some random stranger's home, perhaps in a giant wardrobe large enough to fit two humans and their horses: **Turn to 153**

152 Your horses are at one end of the court, and you and Sam are at the other. And you, my friend, are DEFINITELY winning this little game of tennis.

You glance over at the court beside you, where a man and woman are playing. The woman just returned the man's serve, equalizing the score. The man looks crestfallen, and also really tired. He looks like they've been playing for a long, long while. He looks like he thought he was finally gonna win.

"Tie game," the woman says happily. "What's the matter? Can't quite get the two points you need to beat me and end this game??"

"Just serve the ball," the man says, and she does.

• Hide out here for a bit: I want to see who wins! **Turn to 155**
• Go north: we'll hide in an empty office at City Hall: **Turn to 142**
• Go west: they'll never find us at the beach! **Turn to 154**

153 You make your way down the rows of houses, find one with an unlocked door, and carefully trot your horses inside. There's a man sleeping on the couch, but his house is carpeted, which disguises the noise of your noble steeds. He's got a floor-to-ceiling wardrobe large enough to fit a couple horses and humans inside (fancy!), so you install yourself and Sam inside it, leaving the door open a crack so you can stay aware of what's going on outside.

After a few moments, the man stirs. You're worried that he heard you or your horse cough, but it seems like you're safe: rather than going towards you, he enters the kitchen. You can't see what he's doing, but before long the delicious smell of bacon and eggs is wafting towards you. He's making breakfast in the middle of the afternoon!

This guy is living the friggin' dream!!

Heck, this may not even be his first breakfast TODAY. You kinda want to be this guy. Not gonna lie: I kinda do too.

• Hide out here for a bit: maybe I can learn from him: Turn to 156
• Go north: we'll hide by Verona Dam, a large structure that'll distract passers-by from noticing some random boring people on horses: Turn to 143
• Go east: the beach of the Adige River is just the place to lay low for a while: Turn to 157

154 You blend in with all the couples going for romantic horseback rides on the beach by making sure you and Sam trot in a large loop while saying things like "Oh wow I love you and our relationship, sweetie" and "Let's kiss later, so it's more special" and "We are definitely not wanted men and women trying to look inconspicuous".

You notice a little girl building a sandcastle. She's got the ground level parapets built and is starting work on the second floor. It's a tremendous sandcastle, but you nevertheless have the distinct impression this is merely the largest castle she's built so far TODAY.

You're doing great, little girl!

• Go south, escape the mobs!! Turn to 167
• Hide out here for a bit: this castle is going to be OFF THE HOOK: Turn to 157
• Go north: there's a hill there we could hide behind: Turn to 144
• Go east: the tennis courts there are the perfect place to blend in by playing tennis with our horses: Turn to 158
• Go west: there's some housing there and we could probably hide in some random stranger's home, perhaps in a giant wardrobe large enough to fit two humans and their horses: Turn to 156

155 Your horses are at one end of the court, and you and Sam are at the other. Your steeds are getting the feel of the game, but their returns are still all over the place.

You glance over at the court beside you where a man and woman are playing. The woman has just scored another point on the man.

"And now I'm up by one," gloats the woman. "Match point. That is, unless you care to score a point on me and prolong your agony??"

"Oh, thanks for the invitation, I think I'll take you up on that actually!" the man replies. The woman smiles sweetly, sarcastically, and then slams the ball towards him.

• Hide out here for a bit: I want to see if the man can pull this off! **Turn to 158**
• Go north: we'll hide in an empty office at City Hall: **Turn to 148**
• Go west: they'll never find us at the beach! **Turn to 157**

156 You peek out through a crack in the door to see what's going on outside the safety of your giant, surprisingly spacious wardrobe.

You can't see anyone, but it smells like breakfast and you can hear breakfast noises coming from the kitchen. Suddenly the man exits the kitchen, carrying a frankly amazing plate of eggs and breakfast meat. He sits down on his couch, stares at his meal for a second as if he himself is impressed with how awesome it is, and then carefully dispatches it. Not one crumb is left.

Dang, man. The thought of how good those eggs must've been causes you to take stock of your life. This man just enjoyed a delicious meal in the privacy of his own home, eating happily, without a care in the world. Meanwhile, you're sitting on horseback in a stranger's closet, with a weird butler you barely know beside you, all in the middle of a maze full of angry mobs.

• Hide out here for a bit: maybe he'll show me some of his secrets to his enviable lifestyle and true unblemished happiness: **Turn to 159**
• Go north: we'll hide by Verona Dam, a large structure that'll distract

passers-by from noticing some random boring people on horses: Turn to 146
• Go east: the beach of the Adige River is just the place to lay low for a while: Turn to 160

157 You blend in with all the couples going for romantic horseback rides on the beach by getting down off your horses, giving them some water, lying down on some abandoned beach towels, putting on some abandoned sunscreen, and chilling the heck out.

You notice a little girl building a sandcastle. She's got three storeys built now, and it's literally the most impressive sandcastle you've ever seen. Its size is beyond anything you ever imagined being possible before, and if we're being honest, you've spent a lot of time imagining sandcastles. It looks like she's putting the finishing touches on it now!

Pretty impressive, little girl!

• Go south, escape the mobs!! Turn to 167
• Hide out here for a bit: the castle is almost done and it looks the best ever! Turn to 160
• Go north: there's a hill there we could hide behind: Turn to 111
• Go east: we'll remain inconspicuous on the tennis courts by playing tennis with our horses: Turn to 161
• Go west: there's some housing there and we could probably hide in some random stranger's home, perhaps in a giant wardrobe large enough to fit two humans and their horses: Turn to 159

158 Your horses are at one end of the court, and you and Sam are at the other. They're actually getting . . . pretty good? Your horses might actually beat you, Ophelia.

Maybe that's because you keep glancing over at the court beside you where a man and woman are playing. The man just scored a point on the woman, equalizing their score.

"Oh, too bad, so sad," the man says. "You really thought you were gonna beat me there, huh?"

"Doesn't matter," the woman says. "I can do this all day. And have been, come to think of it." She sighs, tired. "Come on, let's finish this."

Just then, an angry mob approaches from the north, spots you, corner you easily because the tennis court is fenced in, make fun of you for playing tennis with a horse, put a dark bag on your head, and drag you out of there.

Aw man! You didn't even get to see how the match ended!

• Get carried away by the mob: Turn to 163

159 You peek out through a crack in the door to see what's going on outside the safety of your giant, surprisingly spacious wardrobe.

You see a man on a couch, sighing happily. He just ate a really tasty meal. He picks up his plates along with an empty glass, goes into the kitchen, and returns with a giant glass of water.

You lick your lips. That water looks real good right now.

The man sits on his couch and drains the glass in one unbroken swig. Then he puts the glass aside, kicks his legs up on the couch, and lies down. In just a few seconds, he's asleep. There's a smile on his face.

The man doesn't stir from his happy nap, and you can't blame him. Eating a meal, drinking a drink, then having a nap? That sounds REAL NICE. That sounds much nicer than running from angry mobs and hiding in strange houses with a butler and some horses.

• Hide out here for a bit: they'll never find us here! Turn to 150
• Go north: we'll hide by Verona Dam, a large structure that'll distract passers-by from noticing some random boring guy on a horse: Turn to 171
• Go east: the beach of the Adige River is just the place to lay low for a while: Turn to 151

160 You blend in with all the couples going for romantic horseback rides on the beach by loudly saying "YES I TOO HAVE A SWEETHEART AND I LOVE HIM AND WE'RE TOGETHER ALL THE TIME, JUST

NOT RIGHT NOW, BUT IT'S NOT BECAUSE HE DIED BACK IN DENMARK, WHICH IS WHERE I AM FROM", which works reasonably well, all things considered. Nobody cares, Ophelia!

You notice a little girl building a sandcastle. It's tremendous. But just then you hear a rumble of feet and hooves on sand. Looking to the north you see mob running right at you. You try to hide behind the girl's sandcastle, but they plough right through it, reducing it to rubble. They grab you and Sam off your horses and pull bags over your heads.

The little girl doesn't even look up. She just sighs, her hands on her hips, and gets back to the business of rebuilding.

Never change, little girl!

Anyway Ophelia, all you can do now is:

• Get carried off by the mob: Turn to 163

161 Your horses are at one end of the court, and you and Sam are at the other. You're sending serves over to your horses, and I'm not gonna lie, very very few of them are being returned.

You glance over at the court beside you where a man and woman are playing.

"I'm up a point," the man says, bouncing the tennis ball confidently. "One more point and the game's mine."

"Oh, we'll see about that," the woman replies. She crouches into position.

"Come on," she says. "Show me what you got."

• Hide out here for a bit: I want to see if the woman can pull this off! Turn to 152
• Go north: we'll hide inside an empty office at City Hall: Turn to 139
• Go west: they'll never find me on the beach! Turn to 151

162 As you make your way forward, you literally bump into the very obstacle you've been trying to avoid: an angry mob! Here's the bad news: they push you and Sam up against a wall, under such pressure that you both (and a fair number of them) turn into what is most fairly described as a "chunky stew". You're about to say "Wait a minute, I don't understand how you could practically do that, given that w–" but that's as far as you get before you're, as I say, reduced to chunky stew.

• Oh well. Turn to 169

163 The mob dumps you and Sam in a basement, intending to torture you for information. "How did you briefly elude our angry mobs?" they ask. "Normally we kill people on sight, but you managed to, as we say, briefly elude us, and we'd like to know why."

You're super tough and ready for any interrogation they can throw at you, so you give them nothing. Sadly, Sam is not as super tough, and the second they have their enforcer bite off Sam's thumb, he tells them he was just doing what you told him to.

Thanks, Sam.

• Break free and escape: Turn to 166
• Be Sam again, see what's going on with this whole "torture" thing: Turn to 165

164 You swim out to the boat, explain your circumstances to the captain, and are invited to hitch a ride.

"Where are we headed?" you ask, as you climb on board dripping wet.

"Verona," the captain says.

"Aw geez," you say. "So much for my vacation."

But if you're being honest with yourself, you're looking forward to being back in Verona. You wonder how everyone's getting on without you. You wonder what drama you're missing. You go to bed excited about being back on Verona's shores in the not-too-distant future!

• Verona! **Turn to 117**

165 They bit off your thumb, Sam! It's horrible! You're in incredible pain! AHHHHH!!

• AHHHHH!! Being Sam sucks right now, be Ophelia again! **Turn to 166**

166 You, Ophelia, can clearly see where this is going, and so you decide to break free. You trick your captors by asking "what's over there?" and pointing over their shoulders, and when they look, you break free and kill 'em all with just a minor application of your incredibly advanced "kill suckers" skill.

When you free Sam he decides to skip town, and you don't blame him: the dude just got his thumb bit off. Meanwhile, you decide to keep this particular party going, and kill EVERYONE WHO BOTHERS YOU IN VERONA.

Once word gets out about you, you end up killing just about everyone. Turns out this whole town is wound SUPER tight, and there's this weird conflict and endless cycle of revenge between the Montague and Capulet families? And both were represented in the group that captured you, so you've already killed one from each family and basically the whole town hates you now.

Montagues and Capulets alike attack you, and you counter-attack, and like I say you kill pretty much everyone, and the only really interesting thing that happens throughout this is that you come across the corpses of this Montague kid, "Romeo", and this Capulet kid, "Juliet", and it looks like they were SMOOCHING each other as they died. You probably were so busy killing other people when you killed them that you didn't even notice!

You stare at their bodies for a bit, trying to imagine what incredible adventures these two teens could go on if only the timeline were

slightly different, trying to picture the amazing worlds that open up to them if only circumstances were just slightly different.

You start to write down some of your ideas.

• Write a whole book about this: Turn to 168

167 Success!! You and Sam ride into Verona's downtown, safe and secure. He leaves you at a coffee shop, and returns shortly thereafter with papers: some for him that say "SAMUEL AMPSON, BUTLER" and some forged ones for you that read "VIOLENTA STABSWORTH, NON-SUSPICIOUS LADY".

"Violenta?" you say.

"I figured you'd like it," he replies. "Because of how you're so good at violence."

"I am," you say, turning over the papers in your hand. "And I do like it. Thank you."

"What will you do now?" Sam asks.

"Vacation," you say. "Just like we discussed. See the sights of Verona, you know?" And that's what you do.

As Violenta, you check out Verona's museums, their architecture, and their weird obsession with solid-gold statues. And when you're done, you feel like you don't want to go back to Denmark just yet. So you travel some more: to Rome, to England, to Athens, always as Violenta, always learning all you can, enjoying the dizzying sense of freedom that comes with an assumed identity.

Finally you end up in Spain: Rousillon province. There, you get involved in some palace intrigue involving both sick kings AND weird, not unproblematic promises of marriage made by people not even in those marriages, but by keeping your mouth shut, you manage to avoid getting into too much trouble. Everything works out okay! I guess all really IS well that ends well.

When you do finally return to Denmark, it's not to live as a lonely queen presiding over a city of corpses, but to found a new city. A new hamlet, one that doesn't make the same mistakes the old one did. You're going to use your smarts not to efficiently murder more people than have ever been efficiently murdered before, but INSTEAD, wield them to build a new technological and sociological utopia. Disputes will be settled through compromise and mutual understanding instead of stabbing people through curtains. You're going to get it right this time.

And that, Ophelia, is what you do. You change the world.

But before all this happens, before you even arrive back in Denmark, you pass through Verona once more on your way home. And you happen across Sam – remember him? – in some sort of weird argument with other butlers, right there in the middle of the street.

He's biting his thumb at them.

You smile, shrug, and make your way home.

THE END

(. . . or is it?) Turn to 173

P.S. Later on when you're an old lady you die in whichever way you think is the coolest. I recommend: being fired out of a cannon into a volcano!

P.P.S. As you died in absolutely the coolest way possible, this is the happy ending. Congratulations!

P.P.P.S. Sam also didn't die in this run-through either, so: bonus points for that too I guess.

168 You write down all your rad ideas, and a few afternoons later (because that's all the time it takes to write a cool book, don't let anyone tell you otherwise) you have completed your story! You wrote one of those non-linear second-person narrative books, otherwise known as "Choosable Path Adventure" books.

You decide to call your story *Romeo and/or Juliet*. Great title, Ophelia! Now all you need to do is proofread it.

You flip open the cover page of your manuscript and begin to read. "Hello!" your story begins. "I am Ophelia and I am the author of this book. I kinda killed some teens and then I was like, whoah, hold up, what if they didn't die?? So that's what this book is about, all that stuff I thought about when I imagined about that idea. Let me know what you think!!"

That's all there is on page one. You're pretty sure this sounded better when you wrote it.

You turn to page two.

"So who do you want to be in this book?" you read. "Guess what, you can be Romeo or Juliet! Also I was gonna let you play as a cool horse too but then I thought, wait, I'll just never specify that Romeo ISN'T a horse and that way everyone can get what they want!!"

You don't remember writing that last bit at all!

• Play as Romeo: **Turn to 170**
• Play as Juliet: **Turn to 172**

169 Later on scavengers eat the part of the gross body slurry that contained what previously was Sam's thumb, which fulfills a promise I made to him before you even showed up!

You remain extremely dead, and as such, this information makes no impression on you at all.

THE END

(. . . or is it?) **Turn to 173**

P.S. It's just that I promised him his thumb would get bit; it seemed like a good idea at time.

P.P.S. Yes I know that if you'd been aware of the prophecy you would've exploited it by putting Sam in situations in which his thumb getting bit would accomplish things you wanted to see take place! That's why I kept it a secret!!

P.P.P.S. Anyway, you died in what should've been a really easy puzzle for you so I don't know why you're mad at ME

170

"Hey Romeo what is friggin' up??" you read. "By the way, that's you! You're Romeo! You're in love with how a particular human woman – Rosaline – can really STIRRUP your emotions, but oh no she doesn't love you back! You thought you'd have a STABLE life together and that you'd be her MANE man, but instead she looks right PASTURE ('past your') traits, uncaring if that HERDS ('hurts') your feelings!! Now you feel SAD . . . . dle, that is!"

Okay, wow, Ophelia, I really thought you'd write a better book than this. If we're perfectly honest, I thought you'd write a book so brilliant that I could give readers but the barest glimpse of it here, and then everyone would rush out to buy MY book of a similar title. But you've ruined it! You're terrific at science AND murder but you're the absolute worst at writing, and I really wish I'd known this sooner!!

You call me a "neigh-sayer" and it's like, I get it Ophelia, in your book Romeo is a giant horse. Thanks.

Anyway, you've killed everyone in Denmark, Verona, AND my sales, and for that all I can say is I hope it was worth it, OPHELIA.

THE END

(. . . or is it?) Turn to 173

P.S. You were a smelly talking donkey the whole time, SURPRISE

171 As you make your way forward, you literally bump into the very obstacle you've been trying to avoid: an angry mob! Here's the bad news: they attack you and Sam so ruthlessly that they reduce you both to a chunky slurry: smooth in places, weird and lumpy in others. You're about to say "Wait a minute, I don't understand how you could practically do that, given that p–" but that's as far as you get before you're, as I say, slurried all over the place.

• Oh well. Turn to 169

172 "Hi I'm Juliet!" you read. "Actually, I mean YOU'RE Juliet, because that is the character whose choices you're making now! How this works is I'll give you an option and you choose it and then I'll tell you how you die (P.S. you don't always die but usually you do!!!!) Anyway you are a lady who loves a guy named Romeo but you haven't met him yet!! You think it would BEHOOVE you to meet him soon though!! todo: add in a cool story here!!"

That's it. That's literally all it says. Ophelia, you forgot to finish Juliet's story, AND you forgot to not make it suck!! You've really left me in an awkward position here. I THOUGHT your book would get people interested in my book of a similar title and then they'd buy mine instead, but now all I want to do is make sure nobody finds out about your writing ever again!

I go back in time to your Denmark days and make it so you drown off-page in a river for no reason.

THE END

(. . . or is it?) **Turn to 173**

P.S. Oh Ophelia, I can't stay mad at you. You survive the drowning on the condition that you never write fiction again, okay? Okay? Okay. Thanks, Ophelia.

P.P.S. Sorry for introducing time travel on the very last page of this story but as you now know, writing is REAL HARD

173 Well, that's the end of that particular run-through! You, William Shakespeare (that's who you are, remember) close the cover on your book, *How Samuel Ampson Got His Thumb Bit*, and reflect that it certainly is a challenging and experimental story, especially for readers of your previous works, who were maybe expecting something more like *King Lear* or *Macbeth*. You know: serious themes, the fates of nations hanging in a balance – that sort of thing.

It turns out that your suspicions were correct: your latest work actually IS too challenging! Everyone bought a copy because your name was on it, but then none of them really liked it, and so nobody saved their copies and few hundred years later even the fact that you wrote a story about Samuel Ampson getting his thumb bit was forgotten! But fear not, Shakespeare, because one day sufficiently-advanced Shakespeare scholars will be able to recover it by carefully analyzing your life and concluding that this was the sort of thing you'd definitely write, and allowing future generations to one day play the role of the vacationing butler and also maybe the cool science lady from *Hamlet*.

Either way: that was the last book you ever wrote. You die a few days later in a shark-punching incident, and as for the details of how that happened... ah, but that's a story for another time.

(A story for another time which we absolutely included in this book: you just gotta make different choices next time and there'll be a shark to punch! I PROMISE.)

THE END

P.S. Later on in your life you gain access to a time machine and can go back and live your life differently, **turn to 1** to find out precisely how that goes!

CHOOSE YOUR OWN SECOND FOLIO

What you hold in your hands is the first edition of this book – the second and more personalized edition is up to you! Cut these helpful, narrative-altering sentences out of the book and paste them on any previous page, wherever you want. YOU control the narrative! YOU decide what happens! It's arts and crafts, for people who don't mind cutting up some books to make their own fun!

MUSCLE GROUP

Suddenly, your abs flex – a warning sign from your subconscious!

Your pecs flex, involuntarily.

You flex your glutes for emphasis.

Your quads glisten in the moonlight.

You hold everyone's gaze while bouncing your pecs.

But not before you show everyone your cool muscles.

"Flex to meet you!" you shout.

Everyone likes your muscley neck.

You blast your delts.

"Hey. Hey, I've got the best muscles," you announce.

This page intentionally left blank, because we know you're definitely going to cut things out on the other side

> Your lats tense.

> Your giant brain seductively throbs.

> Your regular-sized brain throbs in a way that would be seductive, if it was just a bit bigger.

> Your tiny brain pitiably throbs.

NARRATIVE GROUP

> Just then, you fall into a coma and never wake up! It's a very confusing narrative coma. Turn to page 145 in whatever book you last finished and continue reading from there.

> ...Or WAS it?

> ...Or IS it?

> ...Or DID it?

> ...Or COULD it?

> ...Or DID you?

> P.S. "BEHOLD!" you shout, as you ascend back to your home planet. "I was an immortal alien all along!"

> P.S. You were a ghost this whole time: surprise!!

This page intentionally left blank, because we know you're definitely going to cut things out on the other side

P.S. Everyone ELSE was a ghost this whole time: surprise!!

P.S. This ending must be read ironically.

Just then you wake up. It was all a dream! Crazy! And now, in a twist that makes this entire book fanfiction, you were actually your favourite character in your favourite television show all along! So, that's fun! Suddenly a radioactive spider bites you, which gives you the proportional powers of a spider! You won't use any of these powers during this adventure, but just knowing they're there kinda makes the whole thing cooler nonetheless. You definitely agree that this is the case.

You flirt, gruffly.

You flirt, impatiently.

You flirt, apologetically.

You flirt politely.

You flirt with a quiet empathy.

• Try something different: turn to 174

SPEAKING GROUP

"Daaaaaaang," you whisper.

Friiiiiiig, y'all!

This page intentionally left blank, because we know you're definitely going to cut things out on the other side

You shout some cool obscenities.

You quickly recite the entire text of *Beowulf* to steel yourself. It works! It always does!

You quickly recite the entire text of *Beowulf* to make yourself slightly sleepier. It works! It sometimes does that!

"Wowzers," you mutter through gritted teeth.

"Holla!" you add, significantly.

"Totally," you pant, nodding earnestly.

"GAG ME WITH A SPOON!" you shout, fully at the top of your lungs.

"I know you are, but what am I?" you triumphantly retort.

"My bad," you hiss.

"On second thought," you sigh, "let's not do that..." – but it's already too late.

This only serves to increase your ennui!

This only feeds your sense of dead!

This only feeds your sense that everything's definitely gonna be a-okay!

This page intentionally left blank, because we know you're definitely going to cut things out on the other side

174 *Here's a special choose-your-own ending! Write it yourself!*
Give yourself the happy ending you always deserved, and use the **turn to 174**
cut-and-paste line in the previous section to add a link to it anywhere in the
book you choose!

THE END

(Use this area to illustrate your powerfully audacious and/or horrifying
and/or erotic ending)

BIOGRAPHICAL NOTES

Who created this book, you ask? Well let me tell you, it was:

JOHN ALLISON has been writing and drawing comics since the day he was born in 1976. His initial efforts were rudimentary, but four decades later, he is beginning to grasp the possibilities of the form. John lives in Letchworth in the UK. Illustrator of ending 67.

KORY BING is a an illustrator from Portland, Oregon. She is the creator of the award winning comic series, *Skin Deep*, and the illustrator for Seanan McGuire's *InCryptid* book series. Kory believes anything can be made better with the inclusion of dinosaurs. Illustrator of ending 118.

HANNAH BLUMENREICH is the creator of *Spidey Zine*, and has had work published by BOOM! and Marvel. She lives in Minnesota with a very large cat who has never worked a day in his life. Illustrator of ending 114.

DEREK CHARM is a comic artist and writer living in New York. Once worked on *Jughead* with Ryan North, and they won an Eisner Award for it. Illustrator of ending 30.

MICHAEL CHO is a Canadian illustrator and cartoonist who has drawn lots of stuff for lots of different companies. He often annoys his wife and kids by quoting random bits of Shakespeare (usually *Hamlet*). Illustrator of ending 110.

ANTHONY CLARK is a cartoonist and illustrator from Indianapolis. To answer your followup question, no, he is not the guy from Yes, Dear. You're thinking of Mike O'Malley. You can find more of his work at nedroid.com. Illustrator of ending 13.

TONY CLIFF is the author of the critically-acclaimed, New York Times Bestselling *Delilah Dirk* series of adventure comics. The third, *Delilah Dirk and the Pillars of Hercules*, is on shelves as of August 2018. Grab a warm (or cool!) beverage, put your feet up, and spend some quality time at DELILAHDIRK.COM. Illustrator of ending 173.

JESS FINK is an illustrator and cartoonist. Her graphic novel, *We Can Fix It! A Time Travel Memoir*, is published by Top Shelf. Her erotic Victorian romance comic, *Chester 5000*, has been nominated for an Ignatz award & can be read online. Find all of her work on JessFink.com. Illustrator of ending 76.

MEREDITH GRAN is a cartoonist and comics teacher living in Philadelphia, PA. Illustrator of ending 116.

KC GREEN still draws to this very day. Mostly online. kcgreendotcom.com. Illustrator of ending 32.

CHRISTOPHER HASTINGS is a writer and cartoonist based out of Brooklyn, NY. He's written a lot of fun comics like *Dr. McNinja*, *Gwenpool*, *Adventure Time*, *I Am Groot*, *Guardians of the Galaxy*, *Vote Loki*, *Deadpool*, and *Longshot Saves the Marvel Universe*. He can draw too, I guess. Illustrator of ending 53.

ERICA HENDERSON is the artist of *The Unbeatable Squirrel Girl* for Marvel Comics. She's done lots of other stuff too! But she did *Squirrel Girl* with Ryan so that's what's mentioned here. Illustrator of ending 113.

TYSON HESSE has animated characters on video games like *Skullgirls* and illustrated on comic books like *Diesel*, *Boxer Hockey*, and *Sonic the Hedgehog*. Illustrator of endings 20, 21, 22, 23, 24, 25, 26, 27, 54, 56, 57, 59, 60, 61, and 62.

MIKE HOLMES draws for comics: *Secret Coders*, *Wings of Fire*, *Adventure Time*, *Bravest Warriors*, and *Animal Crackers: Circus Mayhem*. It's pretty fun. Have a great day! Illustrator of ending 95.

ANDREW HUSSIE is the creator of *Problem Sleuth*, which is a comic about detectives, and *Homestuck*, which is a comic about Faygo mostly. Illustrator of ending 14.

JON KLASSEN is an illustrator and author. He has worked for various animation studios and clients but now mostly makes picture books, including *I Want My Hat Back*, *This Is Not My Hat*, and *We Found A Hat*. He is Canadian, but lives in Los Angeles. Illustrator of ending 12.

BRADEN LAMB is a comic artist and colorist. He is partnered in art and life with Shelli Paroline, and together they illustrated Ryan North's *Adventure Time* comics, Arthur Yorinks' graphic novel *Making Scents*, and Ian Lender's picture book *One Day A Dot*. Braden is also the colorist for some of Raina Telgemeier's graphic novels, including *Ghosts* and *The Baby-Sitter's Club* series. Illustrator of ending 172.

DAVID MALKI ! is the author of the comic strip *Wondermark*, which looks a lot like his illustration in this book except with even MORE spooky skeletons, if you can believe that. Illustrator of ending 71.

JAMIE McKELVIE is a British cartoonist and illustrator, best known (so far) for his work on books like *The Wicked + The Divine*, *Phonogram*, and *Young Avengers*. Illustrator of ending 55.

CARLY MONARDO is an artist and performer living in Brooklyn. She has worked behind the scenes on such animated favorites as *The Venture Bros.* and *Steven Universe*, and in front of the scenes as a house performer at NYC's Magnet Theater. Look for her on the streets of the city waving at other people's dogs. www.carlymonardo.com. Illustrator of ending 112.

Frequent Shakespeare collaborator **RYAN NORTH** is the author of two choosable-path Shakespeare books: *To Be or Not To Be* and *Romeo and/or Juliet*. He's also known for his work on *Dinosaur Comics* and *The Unbeatable Squirrel Girl*. He lives in Toronto with his wife Jenn and their dog, Noam Chompsky.

SHELLI PAROLINE escaped early on into the world of cartoons and science fiction, and from there launched into creating comics. She and her husband Braden Lamb form an Eisner Award-winning art team, collaborating on the *Adventure Time* comics and *The Midas Flesh* and *Making Scents*. She lives and works in Salem, Massachusetts. www.shelliparoline.com. Illustrator of ending 170.

RAHZZAH believes in you. Illustrator of ending 64.

MIKE ROOTH is a Canadian Freelance Art Mercenary that has provided thousands of illustrations for books, comics, graphic novels and magazines. He's also the superintendent of a building full time, so when he's not fixing a toilet or scraping vomit off the sidewalk, he's drawing in his 'studio' (living room), enjoying the company of his wife Erika and two cats, Rama and The Bear. Illustrator of ending 66.

ANDY RUNTON is the Eisner Award–winning creator of the breakout all-ages series of graphic novels, *Owly,* starring a kind-hearted little owl who's always searching for new friends and adventure. Spot skulls illustrator.

MARGUERITE SAUVAGE is a French illustrator based in Montréal who has been working in the comics industry for the last 3 years (*Scarlet Witch* Marvel, DC Comics *Bombshells, Adventure Time* Boom Studio . . .). She's also worked as a concept artist, writer and illustrator in various fields like animation, video game, editorial and advertising. Illustrator of ending 80.

SHEN is the cartoonist behind *Owlturd Comix, Bluechair,* and *Live With Yourself.* He does his best, he swears he does. Illustrator of ending 169.

NGOZI UKAZU is the creator of *Check, Please!,* an online graphic novel whose printing campaign remains the most funded webcomics Kickstarter ever. She graduated from Yale University in 2013 with a degree in Computing and The Arts, and received a masters in Sequential Art in 2015 from the Savannah College of Art and Design. Illustrator of ending 167.

CAMPBELL WHYTE lives in the remote Australian city of Perth. He makes comics about the ancient land and the waves of popular culture that wash over it. Illustrator of ending 123.

CHIP ZDARSKY has received many awards but he is also Ryan North's friend, and there is no greater award than that. Take care.